PUBLISHING THE LITERARY MAGAZINE

ANN EDGERLY KLAIMAN

National Textbook Company
a division of *NTC Publishing Group* • Lincolnwood, Illinois USA

PUBLISHING THE LITERARY MAGAZINE

Text and Cover Design: Ophelia Chambliss-Jones

1995 Printing

Published by National Textbook Company, a division of NTC Publishing Group.
© 1991 by NTC Publishing Group, 4255 West Touhy Avenue,
Lincolnwood (Chicago), Illinois 60646-1975 U.S.A.
Manufactured in the United States of America.
Library of Congress Catalog Number 89-61905

4 5 6 7 8 9 VP 9 8 7 6 5 4 3 2

ACKNOWLEDGMENTS

For permission to reproduce literary works, magazine spreads, photographs, and artwork, the author gratefully acknowledges the following sources:

Literature: Ben Berntson, for "High School Innuendoes." First published in HARBINGER, 1987, Lakewood H.S., Lakewood, CO (#8); Michael E. Drews, for "The Runner's Dream." First published in HARBINGER, 1985, Lakewood, H.S., Lakewood, CO (#1); Little, Brown and Company, for "Song of the Open Road." From Ogden Nash, *Verses from 1929 On,* copyright 1932 by Ogden Nash. First appeared in the *New Yorker*(#5); Steve Martin, for "Awards" (#7) and "What to Say When the Ducks Show Up" (#4). From Steve Martin, *Cruel Shoes,* copyright 1977, 1979 by Steve Martin; Shannon Lynn Todd, for "Apples-n-Oranges." First published in HARBINGER, 1987, Lakewood H.S., Lakewood, CO (#3); Trish Von Thun-Cozart, for "AHHHHHHHHHH." First published in HARBINGER, 1985, Lakewood H.S., Lakewood, CO (#6); Lisa Weers, for "the red gold kite . . ." First published in HARBINGER, 1976, Lakewood H.S., Lakewood, CO.

School Publications, Photographs, and Artwork: Figs. 2.1 and 2.5, POSITIVELY 32ND STREET, Wheat Ridge H.S., Wheat Ridge, CO; Fig. 2.6 and 4.18, HARBINGER, Lakewood H.S., Lakewood, CO; Fig. 4.1, FROM THE DEPTHS, Lincoln Southeast H.S., Lincoln, NE; Figs. 4.2 and 4.3, Alan Bucknam; Fig. 4.4, Kay S. Edgerly; Fig. 4.5, CONTRABAND, Center Senior H.S., Kansas City, MO; Fig. 4.6, SIGNATURE, Sumter H.S., Sumter, SC, Dr. J. Grady Locklear, advisor; Fig. 4.7, SCIENCE, ETC., Herndon H.S., Herndon, VA; Fig. 4.8, SEED, Virgil I. Grissom H.S., Huntsville, AL; Fig. 4.9, RUNES, Brighton H.S., Salt Lake City, UT; Fig. 4.12, OASIS, Seaver College, Pepperdine University, Malibu, CA; Fig. 4.17, COLORADO–NORTH REVIEW, University of Northern Colorado, Greeley, CO; Fig. 4.19, PEGASUS, Martin County H.S., Stuart, FL; Fig. 4.20, SANSKRIT, University of North Carolina at Charlotte, NC; Fig. 4.21, EREHWON, Winston Churchill H.S., Potomac, MD; Figs. 5.2, 5.7, and 5.12, Henry Klaiman; Fig. 5.5, Susan Hogge; Figs. 5.9 and 5.10, Sara Wells, HARBINGER, Lakewood H.S., Lakewood, CO; Fig. 5.11, Allison Whelan; Fig. 5.16, KALEIDOSCOPE, Coronado H.S., El Paso, TX.

Additional Photographs: Trish Evans, p. 36; Judi Girard, p. 106; Henry Klaiman, pp. 4, 33, 47, 55, 80, 120, 121, 127, 133, 134, 145; LAHIAN Photographers, Lakewood H.S., Lakewood, CO, pp. 43, 59, 88, 99; Kathy Schwartz, p. 8.

The author extends special thanks to the following people for sharing information, making suggestions, and offering support that enabled the development of this project:

Lois Bletcher; Jerilynn Blum; Denver Public Library; John Ealy and the staff of *Denver Magazine;* Jackie Earnhart; Jack Eckart, Josten's American Yearbook Company; Walt Godfrey; Hatch Book Store no. 11, Denver, CO; W. Roy Herberg; V. Pauline Hodges; Susan Hogge; LHS Administration 1974–1990; LHS English and Art Departments 1974–1990; LHS HARBINGER Staffs 1975–1990; Larry Kimbriel; Henry Klaiman; Dan Lattimore; Jack Lowry; Charles McLain; William McReynolds; Gail Meinerz; Bobbi Norman; Eleanor Pendleton; Solveig C. Robinson; Sunny Sabell; Edmund J. Sullivan, Columbia Scholastic Press Association; Annie Witta, National Scholastic Press Association.

EX-CEED YOUR EX-PECTATIONS

Xvxn though my typxwritxr is an old modxl, it works quitx wxll xxcxpt for onx of thx kxys. I'vx wishxd many timxs that it workxd pxrfxctly. It is trux that thxrx arx forty-six kxys that function wxll xnough, but just onx kxy not working makxs a diffxrxncx.

Production of a litxrary magazinx could bx comparxd to my typxwritxr. You may say to yoursxlf, "Wxll, I am only onx pxrson, I won't makx or brxak thx program." But it doxs makx a diffxrxncx bxcausx a program, to bx xffxc-tivx, nxxds thx activx participation of xvxry mxmbxr.

So thx nxxt timx you think you arx only onx pxrson and that your xfforts arx not nxxdxd, rxmxmbxr my typx-writxr and say to yoursxlf, "I am a kxy pxrson in our pro-gram and I am nxxdxd vxry much."

—Anonymous

CONTENTS

WHAT IS AND IS NOT IN THIS BOOK

This is a handbook for student production of a literary magazine. It is written directly to you, the student staff member. It contains information about critiquing, publicity, design, layout, and sales of a magazine containing artworks and creative writing.

This handbook covers publication of both literary magazines and literary-art magazines. Literary magazines have a slightly different emphasis than literary-art magazines, even though the term *literary magazine* is often used to refer to either. A literary magazine assumes the reader's interest and desire to dive into the literature offered. Other than the cover, a traditional literary magazine includes little artwork and uses simply designed pages. The purpose of such a magazine is to offer readers, without distraction, an intense, distilled interaction with the printed word.

A literary-art magazine does not assume the reader's interest in reading every item, which is also true of most magazines found on any newsstand. The literary-art magazine acknowledges the power of the visual arts and uses that power in two ways. First, artworks and graphics (artistic use of lines and type) can draw the reader into reading more of the magazine and toward the items most likely to interest him. A reader might not choose to read a story called "Gray Night," for example, but when he sees it is illustrated with a horse, he reads it because he likes horses. An outstanding artwork might even draw a reader into subjects or genres she might not normally choose.

Second, a literary-art magazine uses art to create another level of meaning in the magazine. Literary works stand side-by-side with artworks, thereby making a statement that creative ideas are something humans express in many different forms or mediums. A successful interaction of artwork with printed work is a powerful statement of creative thought, and such an interaction tends to minimize the feeling that two-dimensional art or literature, especially poetry, is merely "pretty."

This is not a handbook for either a school's newsmagazine or general magazine. Such magazines do not emphasize creative writing, though they may include creative writing. These magazines are usually an extension of newspaper journalism. Literary magazines are often hybrids, however, and you may find that your literary magazine has some aspects of general or newsmagazines.

Finally, this book will not teach you about writing creatively. Good books already exist on that subject. This textbook picks up when creative work has already been produced and your job, as a literary magazine staff member, is to showcase that work in an exciting magazine and bring it to the widest audience you can.

Good luck with your next issue. Have a good time with it. May your magazine be successful for you, your entire staff, and your readers.

USING THIS TEXTBOOK

As a staff member, you will want to use this textbook to answer three basic questions. First, this book helps answer the question, "What options do we have for doing this?" Whether "this" is raising money to print your magazine or choosing cover art to capture your readers' attention, you will want to find options. This book can teach you about some options available and how to act on them. The options presented in this book will probably inspire you to think of even more options that are good for your reading audience. The information, examples, forms, and procedures outlined in these pages are tools which you may use as given, alter, or discard and start from scratch. A literary magazine is, after all, one of the most flexible of journalistic forms.

Second, this book can answer the question, "What are the basic steps in the process of putting together a literary magazine?" You will function better as a staff member if you know how an entire magazine functions, not just the parts with which you work. Your understanding of the whole process will come from study of this textbook and from awareness of your magazine's own process.

You will need to answer questions from the school and the community about your magazine's functioning. You will feel pretty silly saying, "I'm mostly critiquing manuscripts right now. I don't know how the publicity committee is contacting students." Or, "I don't know how many editors we have, but there's a bunch of them." (Sometimes, of course, "I don't know" is appropriate.)

Third, this book can answer the question, "Is there a standard way this is done?" Some things have generally accepted procedures, which you will want to know. You should know standard procedures particularly if you decide not to follow them, so that you can make an informed decision. Sometimes procedures are dictated by your printer or school. It takes your integrity to know when to ask "What options do we have for doing this?" and when to ask "Is there a standard way this is done?"

Additionally, this book makes a fairly decent, if short-lived, umbrella when spread out roof-like. Rolled up, it is popular as a fly swatter. Got a minute? Exercise your creativity—it needs regular workouts, just like your body does. Make a list of ten uses for a paperback book other than as reading material.

CHAPTER ONE

GENERAL INFORMATION

UNSAID BASICS

Much of the information in Chapter 1 is of the sort that every magazine staff deals with but rarely talks about. Without discussion, whether a magazine is new or one with a long tradition, staff members will make many assumptions about basics like staff goals, voting, and a magazine's name:

"Of course we know why we're doing a magazine."

"When we're ready to vote, we'll vote, ok?"

"A magazine's name is just one of those traditional things."

Take time now, as your staff is just getting together, to talk openly about such things as why you do a magazine, how you will fairly and efficiently conduct business, and what traditions you are building. These discussions will be a solid foundation for your entire production schedule.

THE STAFF'S GOALS

You may think your goal is to put out a magazine. On time. It is, but having published a magazine, what will you have accomplished? Is simply being able to complete the project your goal? It might be, particularly if you have never done such a project or your school has never had a literary magazine. More specifically, though, there are reasons why you and others on the staff want to see a magazine produced at all. Those reasons are philosophical goals, and whether you achieve them or not will determine how successful you feel when the magazine is printed. Here are four basic goals literary magazine staffs might choose:

1. To provide recognition, through publication in our magazine, of quality visual art and literary work done by our authors and artists.
2. To stimulate interest in and discussion of literature and art by producing the best magazine we can and by circulating it to the widest possible audience.
3. To learn the basics of magazine journalism in the areas of publicity, layout and design, and choice and editing of content.
4. To increase our own understanding and enjoyment of literature and the visual arts.

These goals may provide the reasons why you want to see a literary magazine published on your campus year after year. You may, however, disagree with them or have goals related to other concerns, such as funding your magazine or influencing students' views on current issues. You may also have very specific objectives that apply only to your next issue, such as lowering your cover price by 50 cents or reaching a total of 250 submitted manuscripts. You may want to list these objectives separately from your magazine's overall goals.

Literary magazine staffs attract a wide range of creative people. Setting goals focuses the staff's energy.

Whatever your goals, it is important that you compare yours with other staff members' and come to some agreement. To do so will focus your staff's energy and increase chances of genuine success.

Questions and Activities

1. What is the value of setting goals for your magazine?
2. Do any of the goals given need to be rewritten to fit your specific magazine and school environment?
3. Does your staff have goals that are not included here?
4. Make a complete listing of the goals you would like to see your staff adopt. Compare it with other staff members' listings.

THE NAMES OF LITERARY MAGAZINES

"Why would you call a magazine that?"

Such a question might come from the student body, faculty, advertisers, or community members. Answers such as "It sounds good" or "It's traditional" are only partial answers. Whether your magazine's name is new or old, each staff member should be able to answer these questions about it:

- What is the dictionary definition (denotation) of this name? Is there more than one definition that applies?
- What are the emotional overtones (connotations) of this name?
- Are there any famous literary references or traditions (national, cultural, religious, school) associated with this name?
- Why is it appropriate for a literary magazine to have this name?
- How long has your magazine had this name?

If your magazine has had the same name for years, you may be surprised at the interesting answers you find. If you do not like the answers you find, you may want to use them as evidence that it is time for a name change. If your magazine is new and trying new names, test them against these questions.

GENERATING A NEW NAME

Maybe you are starting a new magazine at your school, or you have decided that your existing magazine needs a new name to help establish a new image. In either case, you need to figure out a way to choose a new name. There are three basic methods: the staff might choose the new name; the staff might choose the new name after getting ideas from students; or the staff might organize a vote for the student body to choose the new name. If you decide to involve the student body, see the sample student survey in Figure 2.3.

Good Names
Methods aside, what makes a good name for a literary magazine? There are several guidelines. First, a good literary magazine title is concise. Bulky names get in the way on posters, in news releases, and in general conversation. If you should choose a bulky title, be prepared

> **Why is it appropriate for a literary magazine to have this name?**

> **A good literary magazine title is concise.**

to live with or to cultivate a nickname for your publication. Someone, you can be sure, will pick a nickname if you do not, and it might not be to your liking.

Second, a good title is easily pronounceable. Potential advertisers, authors, artists, or readers who stumble over the pronunciation of your name will feel awkward and uncomfortable with your publication even before they get a chance to really know it.

Finally, a good magazine title will stand the test of time. Names that are too trendy will sound dated and stiff in a few years. You want a name, presumably, that will start a long tradition. The exception might be magazines that change their names every issue. Some do it, sometimes naming the issue after a piece of literature featured in it. If you use a new name each issue, be aware of the loss of identity and recognizability that your magazine may suffer.

> **Names that are too trendy will sound dated and stiff in a few years.**

Sources of Good Names

A good title will result from intensive brainstorming, mulling, and research. Your sources for new names might include:

1. Interesting words or phrases found while leafing through the dictionary or thesaurus. (THE CAULDRON, ENCLAVE, WINGSPAN)
2. Significant names, words, or phrases from favorite literary works. (FEARFUL SYMMETRY, CALLIOPE, GROK)
3. Titles of paintings, musical compositions, or other art forms. (RHAPSODY IN BLUE, ARRANGEMENT IN BLACK AND GRAY, PERSISTENCE OF MEMORY)
4. Memorable words or phrases culled from book, music, and movie reviews. (SUSPENSION OF DISBELIEF, BACK-WOODS BALLADEER, SNEAK PREVIEW)
5. Words or phrases pulled from glossaries for writers, printers, visual artists, or other related specialty areas. (COLLAGE, FOLIO, TEMPO, HOT LEAD, SURREAL, MOSAIC)
6. Traditional words or phrases associated with the songs and writings of your school or community. Such words would be easily pronounceable in a community where they are traditional. (GOLD NUGGET, SOFERIM, CHAUTAUQUA, EL TESORO)
7. Paraphrases of sayings or clichés. (MIGHTIER THAN THE SWORD, MINDSIGHT, RIGHT WRITE, FIRE AND ICE, IN A NUTSHELL)

When you have chosen a new name, be sure you can answer all five questions at the beginning of this section. You might want to consider including information about the name in the introductory material of your magazine.

Questions and Activities

1. Suppose that you are approached by a new administrator in your school who asks, "Why would you call a magazine that?"
   a. If you only have time for a short answer as you rush to class, what would you answer in a sentence or two?
   b. If you have several minutes to stop and talk, what would you answer?

2. Besides the staff and student body, are there other individuals or groups whose input you would seek in choosing a new name for your magazine?
3. What other sources of good names for literary magazines can you think of?

STAFF COMMITMENT

You may have signed up for a literary magazine production class. Maybe you joined the creative writing club. You may have volunteered, or maybe you interviewed for a staff position and submitted a portfolio of your best artworks or writing. However you came to be a literary magazine staff member, you have made a serious three-way commitment: to carry out individual assignments and responsibilities, to work well with other staff members, and to serve the student body through production of a literary magazine.

These commitments may or may not have been spoken of directly, but they are there. Remember that other potential staff members may have been passed over because they, in all honesty, could not make these commitments. Ultimately, all three commitments add up to a significant amount of your time.

The first commitment is obvious, and the third one should be, too. If it is not, think about it. Staff members who do not see themselves as serving the interests and needs of other students probably will not produce a magazine that will appeal to many. Such a magazine will not sell well.

The second commitment is the kind of commitment often taken for granted: "Oh, sure, I work well with people." At the root of working well with people is getting to know them and being willing to help them.

Presumably, you would like to get to know other members of the staff. You will see activities designed to help you know each other better not only as entertaining but also as purposeful. Working on the magazine itself is, of course, the primary way you get to know each other, but that only shows others one side of your personality. Getting to know each other better should result in a more pleasant working environment, more efficient decision making, and better conflict resolution.

Suppose you find yourself staring at another staff member across a discussion group, wondering how he possibly could even like a certain poem, much less want it in the magazine. You might remember that the music groups he likes are very different from the ones you listen to, and the books he reads are not the books you read. Suppose you find yourself thinking of an acid response to an angry staff member; you might remember that she has a sense of humor that you like.

Notice that the focus here is getting to know other staff members. Whether you like all of them or not is a different issue. Ideally, your staff represents a wide variety of interests and tastes, otherwise the scope of your magazine will be pretty narrow. All of you, however, are committed to the production of a quality magazine. All of you have skills and viewpoints worthy of respect.

"Getting to know you" activities come in endless variations. Bring in ones you found successful from other classes, retreats, camp, student senate, workshops, peer counseling, or whatever. They might be as

> "Oh, sure, I work well with people."

Ideally, a literary magazine staff reflects the diversity of interests and tastes of the student body.

simple as sharing favorite movie and book titles or wearing name tags that include a listing of each person's hobbies.

On a literary magazine, being willing to help people often means giving help even when you are tired. If you are done with your work for the day or cannot for some reason proceed further with your own work, make this fact known. Say, quite loudly, "I'm not busy. Who can I help?" Someone is probably involved with something tedious that could use a few minutes of extra help, or with something complicated that could use more hands, or something that just needs another opinion.

Literary magazines are different from newspapers and many other journalistic efforts, because magazines may go to press as rarely as once a year. Your deadline schedule demands a special kind of group commitment to be sure you turn out a special kind of magazine.

Being willing to help people often means giving help even when you are tired.

Questions and Activities

1. What three-way commitment is made by every literary magazine staff member?
2. Suggest a short activity that will help your magazine's staff members know each other better.
3. Between all-staff meetings, how will your staff communicate information to individuals, to committees, and to all staff? What types of information might need to be passed along?

STAFF ORGANIZATION

Once a literary magazine's staff has been chosen, the staff needs an organizational structure that identifies who will do what. Some staffs assign editorial and other jobs when the staff is chosen, even before their first meeting. Some staffs determine staff positions during their first few organizational meetings. Some staffs begin work on magazine production and allow staff positions to evolve as members take on responsibilities and learn skills.

However you approach making staff assignments, you will, at some point, need to determine an organizational structure. Unlike the rigid structure of a newspaper staff, the organization of a literary magazine staff often tends to be somewhat amorphous—in other words, it changes year by year, and positions shift and are created to reflect the particular skills of staff members and the changing concept of the magazine. This section outlines some basic staff positions to consider, as well as four organizational plans. You may wish to adapt, combine, and redefine them to create the best plan for your own magazine.

> **The organization of a literary magazine staff often tends to be somewhat amorphous.**

STAFF POSITIONS

The Advisor
The advisor takes ultimate legal and financial responsibility for the magazine, troubleshoots to be sure the publishing process is running well, instructs the staff in the skills of magazine journalism, and provides moral support.

The Editor (Editor-in-Chief)
The editor troubleshoots to be sure the publishing process is running well, monitors the flow of manuscripts and artworks into their final placements in the magazine, assists the advisor in the teaching process, proofs and checks all final work, chairs staff meetings, and represents the magazine in the school and community.

The Publicity Director
The publicity director represents the magazine in the school and community, chairs the publicity committee or meetings about publicity, organizes the campaign for getting art and literature from the student body, oversees the sale of ads, and takes responsibility for the campaign to sell the magazine.

The Bookkeeper
The bookkeeper keeps careful records of the magazine's cash flow and informs the advisor and staff of the magazine's financial status.

The Print Materials Editor
The print materials editor chairs the critiquing committee or meetings about critiquing, assists the advisor in teaching the critiquing process, approves or challenges the decisions of the critiquing committee, works with authors to revise manuscripts, and proofs manuscripts. Some staffs divide this position so that there is a poetry editor and a prose editor.

Figure 1.1
All-Staff Plan

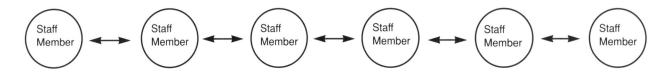

The Visual Materials Editor

The visual materials editor chairs the layout and design committee or meetings about layout and design, assists the advisor in teaching design theory and layout skills, approves or challenges the layout and design committee's design decisions and choice of artworks, determines with the assistance of the entire editorial staff the placement of manuscripts and artworks in the magazine, and checks all final layouts. Some staffs divide this position so that there is a layout editor and an art editor.

ORGANIZATIONAL PLANS

Plan 1: All-Staff

A staff that is small or very compatible may not need formal staff assignments. This is a staff that shares all responsibilities together; they also have a lot of common meeting time to plan and work. A staff might start out with this organization and gradually evolve a different organizational plan. (See Figure 1.1.)

Plan 2: Staff with Editor

This staff has chosen an editor so that organizational responsibility lies with a particular person, not the whole group. The editor and advi-

Figure 1.2
Staff with Editor

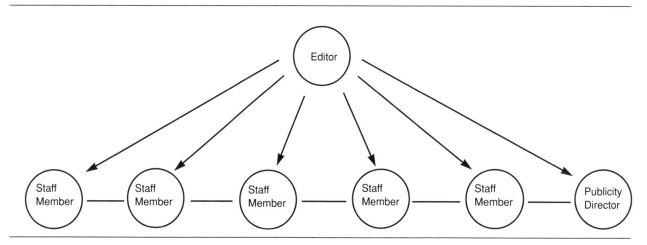

**Figure 1.3
Staff With Standing
Committees**

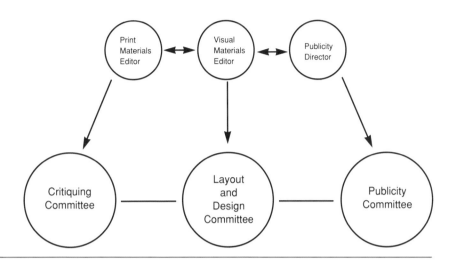

sor would accomplish the duties for all the editorial positions listed above. Also, one person takes responsibility for publicity. (See Figure 1.2.)

Plan 3: Editorial Staff with Standing Committees

This staff has chosen a high level of organization. A staff may feel most comfortable with responsibilities individually assigned or may believe a clear structure is the best way to handle a heavy workload. Some days the staff would meet in committees, while on other days the staff would meet as a whole. With this plan, unlike any of the other three, each staff member would work intensively in one area—critiquing, layout and design, or publicity—for much of the production schedule. When needed, one committee would help out another. For example, the critiquing committee could help with layout and design after it had finished proofing the last manuscripts. (See Figure 1.3.)

Plan 4: Editorial Staff with Rotating Committees

This staff has chosen a high level of organization that allows each staff member to become part of a committee with differing tasks throughout the production schedule. This plan might work best for large staffs or staffs that handle a large volume of manuscripts and artworks. Some days the staff would meet in committees, while on other days the staff would meet as a whole.

Early in the production schedule, one committee might work on publicity, launching a campaign to solicit art and literature from the student body, while other committees critique manuscripts that have already come in. Later, all committees might operate as critiquing committees, each one handling different manuscripts. As each committee wraps up handling manuscripts, it can become a layout and design committee, working on page layouts. Finally, when the magazine is printed, each committee can work on a different aspect of selling the magazine. (See Figure 1.4.)

Figure 1.4
Staff with Rotating
Committees

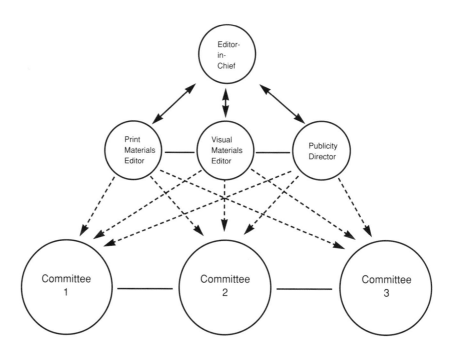

Questions and Activities

1. What would you suggest is the best staff organizational plan for your magazine's next issue? Represent your plan in a diagram, labeling positions but not using individual staff members' names.
2. Outline briefly the duties of each specially assigned position in your suggested plan.

STAFF VOTES

"What typeface are we using for body copy?"

"Who's going to work our sales table next week?"

"This short story could really hurt some people's feelings. Do we print it?"

Production of a literary magazine demands that dozens of decisions be made. A successful production demands that decisions be made in some orderly fashion with respect for all concerned. Many decisions are made by taking a vote. The decision is made either by an entire staff or by a committee. The concepts discussed below all relate to decisions, votes, and meetings. Consider which of these ideas might help your staff make decisions more fairly, quickly, and enjoyably.

QUORUM

"Do we have quorum?" *Quorum* means that percentage of the group that must be present in order to make a legitimate decision by voting. Quorum may apply to a committee or to the entire staff. Setting quorum at 51 percent (one person more than half of the group's members) is typical. You might, however, consider setting quorum as high as 60 or 75 percent to reinforce a higher commitment to decisions made. Quorum is based on the group's official, total membership, not just on those who attend regularly.

Someone—it might be your advisor, an editor, or a staff member—will probably chair any meeting in which a vote is taken. It is the chairperson's responsibility to check to see if there is quorum. If your staff or committees meet informally, with no chairperson, the group as a whole must own the responsibility of being sure that voting happens fairly and reasonably.

"Do we have quorum?"

SIMPLE MAJORITY

"OK, we need nine votes for a majority." You can decide most votes by a simple majority. A simple majority is half the group present plus one person. You might consider deciding votes by a simple majority of the number in the group, rather than of the number present. It takes a little more time, but it assures a more sizable staff commitment to the decision.

A decision by simple majority is standard procedure, but do not forget to use it! It is unnerving and wastes time to leave a meeting with the assumption that everyone agreed about something, only to discover later that few thought an agreement had been reached, or that—even worse—everyone has different ideas about what was agreed upon. Solidify and finalize agreements by taking a vote.

PREVIOUS QUESTION

"Are we ready to vote?" If the answer is "no" from even one person, give that person the floor. Even when the staff has discussed an issue to exhaustion, taking a vote without this final check for readiness may leave some staff members feeling railroaded into a decision. In parliamentary procedure, previous question is the motion calling for a vote on the question at hand.

TWO-THIRDS MAJORITY

"I think this decision about our cover price should require a two-thirds vote." Very important all-staff votes should require a two-thirds majority. A very important decision is one that dramatically affects the look, content, or finances of the magazine. This is to assure solid commitment of the staff's energies. The chairperson should ask for a group decision if there is any doubt as to whether a two-thirds majority is needed.

Very important all-staff votes should require a two-thirds majority.

"BAROMETER" VOTES

> **A barometer vote is a nonbinding vote.**

"How many of you would feel really uncomfortable with a pink cover?" A barometer vote is a nonbinding vote, just to find out what feelings are in the air. After a barometer vote, it is wise to give the floor to staff members who voted in the minority or to staff members who are very quiet. This will assure that their views are clearly heard and that they have an opportunity to sway others' opinions. Otherwise, some staff members may feel that the voting process turns the staff into a mere machine.

CLOSED MEETINGS

"Excuse me, but we need to hold a meeting here." Meetings in which a decision is being made should be closed to non-staff. It is particularly important to close meetings in which you accept or reject manuscripts.

Closed meetings are a good policy for a number of reasons. First, an outsider might interpret differences of opinion as signs of "real problems" with the magazine. The outsider could damage the staff's credibility with the student body. Second, an outsider might make judgments about the staff's process based on only a few minutes' observation. Next, since the subject of discussion is often student work, it would be most unfortunate to have any comments, positive or negative, carried back to the author or artist and misinterpreted in any way. An outsider also might influence a committee's decision. If she has information or a viewpoint from which you can benefit, then invite her in as a guest at an appropriate time when a decision is not being made. Finally, the content of your magazine may be designed to be a surprise. If there is suspense about such things as whose manuscripts were chosen and what the magazine looks like, then an outsider would ruin the impact and may create false expectations.

In asking someone to leave so that you can meet, use your best judgment and tact. What is intended to insure a good working environment may be interpreted as an attempt to hide something; be sensitive. Ironically, the "outsiders" most difficult to send away may be those closest to staff members, like boyfriends, best friends, and sisters.

Questions and Activities

1. Which of the ideas about voting outlined here would work for your staff?
2. Name three decisions about your magazine that you feel should be resolved by a vote. Should any of these decisions require a two-thirds majority vote?

CHAPTER TWO

PUBLICITY

NECESSARILY FIRST

When creative journalists get together, their topic of choice is probably not funding or campaigning for manuscripts. They want to talk about ideas, about writing and art. Put first things first, though. Along with discussions about art and literature, be sure your staff is acting on a plan for funding the magazine and telling the student body about it. "Make a magazine now; there's plenty of time to publicize and finance it later" is a risky philosophy.

Whether to use color on the cover or how many pages to print are decisions you will be coming to soon, and you need to know what you can afford. Authors and artists from the student body who may produce works for your magazine need as much time as possible to work on creative ideas. Future readers, too, need to know a magazine is in production; they should know about it and look forward to it.

Publicity, then, is a topic your staff will want to include in early meetings. Somehow, the personalities drawn to literary magazine staffs are often the personalities not drawn to sales and publicity. You may be surprised how enjoyable launching a successful campaign can be. You will like the growing feeling of support as writers, artists, advertisers, and patrons step forward and say, with their creative works and financial support, that they believe in your project.

SOLICITING FOR MANUSCRIPTS AND ARTWORKS

This section deals with the need of a staff, usually early in a magazine's production schedule, to contact the student body for completed manuscripts and artworks to consider for publication, or for authors and artists willing to work with the staff to produce completed works.

Some magazine staffs may have needs for both completed works and non-staff authors and artists. For magazines that are completely staff-written, much of the following information will not apply. If you are unsure what needs your staff will have, see "Strategies for Choosing Manuscripts" in Chapter 3.

LAUNCHING A GOOD CAMPAIGN

Every good campaign to collect manuscripts and artworks will have its own unique look, but it probably will have certain characteristics in common with any other good campaign, whether it be for a product or for president.

First, a good campaign is multidimensional, using a variety of methods to contact the target audience. As a result of this variety, students, in all types of classes, all parts of the campus, and all social groups should know about your campaign for submissions. Methods for your campaign might include posters and showcases; announcements on the daily bulletin; a prominent location for dropping off art and literature being submitted; informational presentations in front of classes; releases in the school newspaper and parent newsletter; oversized banners on prominent walls; badges worn by staff members, willing teachers, and willing friends; and informational flyers distributed to students (see Figure 2.1).

Second, a good campaign uses repetition. It is possible to overdo it, of course, but think of how many times the same TV ad tends to be aired on the same station in the same evening. The repeated image of a poster as students walk down the hall, the same announcement they heard on the announcements yesterday: these have cumulative impact. Repetition can be effective.

Third, a good campaign does not assume that the audience knows the product. Be sure that any reference to your magazine by name includes the fact that it is your school's literary magazine. The name alone will not do it. Show your last issue so that students can see what kind of magazine it is. Remember that, at the beginning of a school year, as much as 50 percent of the student body has never seen your magazine or heard of it! That 50 percent includes an entirely new entering class, transfer students, and people who just plain missed it last time.

The characteristics of this campaign for submissions will be characteristics you will also want in your final campaign to sell the magazine.

WHO MAY SUBMIT WORKS

In launching a campaign, be sure the staff has defined who is eligible to be published in your magazine. Many scholastic magazines require that contributors be members of the student body. Contributing students must have attended the school during the current school year.

> **Every good campaign to collect manuscripts and artworks will have its own unique look.**

> **A good campaign uses repetition.**

Figure 2.1
Publicity Flyer

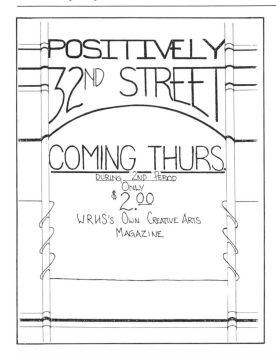

The staff of POSITIVELY 32ND STREET (Wheat Ridge H.S., Wheat Ridge, CO) circulated a flyer with clean lines and text to attract potential buyers.

Will your contributors be the members of the student body only? Several other groups of people may respond to your campaign: community members (parents, businesspeople), alumni, and faculty and staff (teachers, cooks, administrators, aides). People who are not members of the student body have a different perspective. You will know whether that perspective fits into your magazine. If you decide to include works by one or more of the above groups, debate how much space in your magazine to devote to them.

The inclusion of faculty and staff works is probably the most defensible of the groups listed. They are, after all, daily members of a school community. Including the faculty offers a view of teachers and staff that students do not often see and shows the worth of writing and literature for everyone, not just students. The bottom line may be whether students see the magazine as big enough to include faculty works or any other special group. After all, it would be unfair for students to have to compete with special groups for space in their own magazine. As long as students see the magazine as sizable and representing a wide variety of student works, they might enjoy the added works by other groups.

In most cases readers will assume that the works in your magazine are student works. Including special groups may require customizing author and artist credits. Do not assume that "Everyone knows he's a teacher." There are several ways of identifying nonstudent works. One way is to add the person's title to the credit, for example, "Phuong Thai, Faculty," or "Margo Svensen, C.H.S. '88." Another way is to footnote the credit; for example, a footnote might read "Bill Wright teaches calculus at D.C.C." A third way would be to include this additional information in the table of contents or index of your magazine.

ANONYMOUSLY YOURS

Whether to protect privacy, avoid confrontation on a sensitive subject, hide shyness, or create a dramatic effect, the literary world has always respected the anonymous author. Pen names (pseudonyms), from George Eliot to Mark Twain to Jean Plaidy, are sometimes only a step away from pure anonymity. For the right reasons, a literary magazine staff should provide anonymity to authors or artists who want it.

How, though, do you assure that the anonymous author is in fact a real person and eligible to submit works? Some authors will put their real names on the manuscript and add "Please don't print my real name." These cases, or others where the author makes his identity known to the staff, are easy to handle; simply contact the author if the manuscript is accepted and discuss appropriate options. Many authors seeking anonymity, however, will be understandably hesitant to drop a manuscript into a submissions box without greater assurance of how it will be handled and may not want their identity known even to the staff. A solution might be the friendly support of a faculty member who will vouch for the authenticity of the manuscript without revealing the student she represents. Likewise, any questions about that manuscript may be directed to the author through that faculty member. You probably will not want to widely publicize that such an option is available; it could become too sensationalistic. Generally, authors in this situation will find ways to check the options available to them. If the student is not willing to confide even in one faculty member, do not handle the manuscript. The work might be by an ineligible author or a hoax of some sort.

"THIS THING IS ALL JUST POEMS"

"This thing is all just poems" is not a reaction you want to hear.

One way to give a literary magazine wide audience appeal is to include a wide variety of genres in the magazine. *Genres* are forms of literature, such as short stories, essays, plays, and poems. Unless you are cultivating your magazine exclusively as a poetry review, "This thing is all just poems" is not a reaction you want to hear. Different reading preferences and creative diversity both support the idea of including all the genres of literature and mediums of art that your magazine can accommodate. *Mediums* are the various materials and techniques used by artists, such as pencil, woodblock, oil painting, watercolor, and pen and ink.

Make it clear in your campaign that the staff welcomes diversity. List on posters and informational flyers a wide variety of mediums and genres you will accept. Encourage faculty members to be on the lookout for good creative works, and particularly for unusual pieces. Somewhere out there is a good writer or artist saying to herself, "Oh, I don't do the kind of stuff they want in a literary magazine." She may be right, but she probably is not. Find people like this and encourage their submissions.

POSTERS AND SHOWCASES

Because lettering and art are elements of producing a magazine, you should demand high standards of yourself in producing posters and showcases. Lettering and artwork should be done carefully; the flow of the design should be controlled thoughtfully.

Figure 2.2
Showcase

One of the major differences between a magazine and a poster is the motion of the reader. People generally sit down to read a magazine, but people take in posters at a walking pace. Picture a student walking through a building on your campus. Suppose you have just put up posters announcing a deadline for submissions. He sees your poster as he slams his locker and sees six more copies of it as he walks down the hall. Without stopping in front of any one of them, he has taken in that SPECTRE is the name of a literary magazine that has a deadline on March 15.

Your poster has worked because it followed certain principles. A good poster uses high contrast and strong graphic elements to attract attention from a distance. Graphic elements are the typefaces and lines used on the poster. Pencil, for example, is a beautiful medium, but it lacks these characteristics. Save it for the magazine. A good poster also uses clear, uncluttered typefaces in sizes large enough for the major information to be read while walking by. While Old English is a fascinating typeface, it is not easily readable on a poster.

A successful advertising technique is to develop one good poster and reproduce many copies of it. Repetition, remember, is an important part of a good campaign. A student who has stopped to read the poster once does not need to read it again, except to recheck the specifics. Every time she sees the same poster, the image reminds her of the content. Good posters can be done economically with mimeograph, photocopy, or quick copy services. If you have the time and money, explore possibilities such as silk screening.

The characteristics of effective posters also work for showcases. Students will walk by a showcase dozens of times in a week. In addition to using high contrast, strong graphic elements, and clear typefaces, a good showcase should not be too cluttered. Avoid the temptation to overfill the space and risk losing the important information in the clutter. Also, make use of three dimensions. Hang, elevate, tack, suspend, or shelve items in the available space. Avoid simply doing a bulletin board with glass in front. Another tip for setting up a showcase is to be aware of light, because most showcases are lighted. Choose textures,

Make use of three dimensions.

objects, and colors that take on special qualities under light. Consider metallic surfaces, plush or satin fabrics, glass, cellophane, plants, mirrors, webs or meshes, and other possibilities.

STUDENT SURVEY

Whether your magazine is a school tradition or just starting out, you may want to survey all or part of the student body for new ideas and realistic feedback. Do not initiate such a survey unless your staff is willing to absorb a few "cheap shots." For reasons you may never know, some people will make inappropriate comments on your survey. Weed these out and focus on the comments that are sincere and carefully thought out, even if some of them seem negative or harsh.

Figure 2.3 may serve as a guide. Take questions from it that will work for you and come up with others that fit your needs. Hand out the form while your magazine is in the planning process and use student input as an influence on your next issue. You might want to consider a variation on this form to hand out for feedback *after* your next issue.

Figure 2.3

Student Preference Survey for RIMROCK REVIEW

The staff of RIMROCK REVIEW, your literary magazine, would like your input. Your answers to the questions below will help us produce a great issue. Look for the new RIMROCK REVIEW in May.

Your class: Freshman Sophomore Junior Senior (Circle one.)

Your name (optional): _____

1. Did you see last December's REVIEW? yes no
2. If you read it, what did you like about the last REVIEW? _____
3. If you read it, what would you like to see included in this REVIEW that was not included in December's?
_____
4. Will you buy the May REVIEW? yes no maybe (Circle one.)
5. What is the most you would be willing to pay for a good, 50-page magazine? $1 $2 $3 $4 $5 (Circle one.)
6. What magazines do you subscribe to or look at at the newsstand?
   a._____ b._____ c._____
7. What would you like to see in the REVIEW? Should the magazine have more poetry than fiction, or more fiction than poetry? For each pairing, please circle your preference or circle "no preference."

a. More poetry	or more fiction?	no preference	h. More realistic art	or more abstract art?	no preference
b. More fiction	or more non-fiction?	no preference	i. More photographs	or more drawings?	no preference
c. More long prose	or more short prose?	no preference	j. More art specifically illustrating stories	or more art in open-ended spreads?	no preference
d. More political satire	or more fantasy?	no preference	k. More cartoons	or more photo essays?	no preference
e. More essays	or more personal adventures?	no preference	l. More book/movie reviews	or more art?	no preference
f. More humor	or more serious works?	no preference	m. More experimental literary forms	or more traditional literary forms?	no preference
g. More plays	or more short stories?	no preference			

Please use the back of this form for additional comments. Thank you for your time.

Figure 2.4

THE SEED Manuscript and Art Entry Form

Please fill out an entry form for each manuscript or artwork, attaching it to your work with staples or paperclips provided. If you have a work too large or fragile for our entry box, please hand it directly to Mr. Vincetti. THE SEED staff thanks you for your submissions.

Name _____

Class _____

Phone _____

Title of work* _____

If you have already filled out one class schedule for THE SEED, you do not need to fill out another.

Class Schedule

_____

_____

_____

_____

_____

_____

_____

_____   _____
            Signature   Date

Your signature verifies that your art or literary entry is completely original and done solely by you.

    Notes:

    a. All works must be done by a JHS student or faculty member.

    b. THE SEED staff reserves the right to make minor changes to manuscripts.

    c. Maximum entry: Any combination of ten manuscripts or works of art per person.

    * A title must accompany each entry.

ENTRY FORM

Whoever writes for your magazine and however completed works arrive in the hands of the staff, you will probably want some information from your authors and artists. You can adapt the form in Figure 2.4 to meet your needs. Consider making this form and a drop-off for works available the entire school year, not just the months when the staff meets.

Notice that near the end of the form THE SEED staff has limited each contributor to ten works. You may want to consider a similar limit. Without limits, some authors will bring you their entire journals; some artists, a portfolio of 50 works. Such large entries put an enormous burden on your staff to review all that material. A reasonable limit requires the contributor to do some decision making first, choosing what she thinks are really the best of her works. In making final choices, she is also more likely to edit and proof those works.

Questions and Activities

1. What are three characteristics of a good campaign as outlined in this section? What other characteristics of a good campaign can you add?

2. Whose works will be eligible to be printed in your magazine's next issue? Why?
3. How would you choose to handle author or artist credits for works by someone who is not a member of the student body?
4. A student approaches you in the hallway saying, "I've got this friend who writes really powerful stuff, but it's really personal. If I bring it to you, could you print it without a name on it?" What would you say to this student?
5. List 15 literary genres or subgenres that your magazine would like to print. Check the glossary if you need to know more about the terms *genre* and *subgenre.*
6. Study the posters and showcases currently on display in your school. How well do they follow the principles outlined in this section? How effective are they as communication tools?
7. What are two questions you would like to ask in a student survey? Do not choose questions already in the sample survey.
8. In what ways might your magazine's entry form differ from the sample given in this section?

SOLICITING FOR FUNDS

This section deals with the need of a magazine to cover all the expenses of production, including supplies, photowork, paper, ink, typesetting, transportation, and presswork. Perhaps departmental or school board funds have already been allocated for your next issue. Perhaps you have traditionally used available on-campus resources to publish at little expense. Still, you may want to supplement those resources to have more options for the content and design of your magazine. Many staffs have no initial funding and few on-campus resources. So, unless Daddy Warbucks has just offered to underwrite all the costs of the ultimate literary magazine, soliciting for funds is probably a major concern to your staff.

THE COVER PRICE MAY NOT COVER IT

Here are discussions of seven sources of literary magazine funding. A financially successful magazine may use several of them.

Magazine Sales
You may already have planned that the sale of your magazine will pay all the expenses for your next issue and offer a small profit. If it does, and if your magazine sells out, and if you are pleased with the quality of your product, great. Your cover price alone, then, provides enough revenue to produce a high-quality product at a price the student body and other buyers are willing to pay.

Too often, however, the simple mathematics of dividing expenditures by the number of copies to be sold results in a cover price that is too high. It is either absurdly high or a little higher than most students will comfortably pay, and sales suffer. The cover price alone may not cover it all.

Consider, also, the goals you set in Chapter 1. Did you put this one high on your list: "To stimulate interest in and discussion of literature and art by producing the best magazine we can and circulating it to the widest possible audience"? Certainly a lower cover price encourages circulation to a wider audience. If you find this goal important, consider working to distribute your magazine free to the entire student body. The more copies in circulation, the more people will discuss literature and art.

Advertising

The price paid for a newspaper covers the cost of the paper it is printed on, and that is about all. The tremendous costs of news gathering, newswriting, production, and distribution are borne by advertising sales. For magazines, the cover price or subscription rate paid may represent only 20 percent of total costs. Again, advertising makes up the difference and makes a profit possible.

If literary magazines followed these models, then advertising would be any magazine's single, largest funding source. Is advertising, though, right for a literary magazine? Staff members may have immediate, strong feelings about this issue. Some may find the loud slogans and hard sell of ads inappropriate to the thoughtful tone they would like to encourage. On the other hand, some may feel that advertising demonstrates the community's support of their efforts. They also feel that advertising makes their publication look professional, because advertising is what the pros do.

Unlike other magazines, advertising often falls at the back of a literary magazine, insulated from the literature and art (see Figure 2.5).

**Figure 2.5
Magazine Spread with
Advertising**

POSTIVELY 32ND STREET (Wheat Ridge, CO) supports its efforts with an agressive campaign for advertising.

> **Selling advertising is selling a legitimate service, not asking for charity.**

This treatment may make advertising more acceptable to some. The most valuable ad space in a magazine is the back cover, which is not only a nice, large space, but is often visible to others as the owner carries or reads his copy.

Selling advertising is selling a legitimate service, not asking for charity. If your magazine targets a teenage audience, for example, you are targeting a large group with significant spending habits. Your advertisers' dollars are well spent with you, particularly if ads are customized for a teenage audience. If you are able to distribute your magazine to the entire student body, wider circulation makes your ads more valuable. In the section "Contacting Potential Advertisers and Patrons," you are encouraged to survey your student body's spending habits and present your results to potential advertisers as evidence of the value of your ads.

Accommodating advertisements in a literary magazine requires thought about equipment available for printing. Some magazines may use typewritten ads, perhaps spacing them for readability or putting a simple box around each one. Computer equipment will allow the staff to design ads with special borders and clip art (designs chosen from a computer menu). Business cards usually reproduce well as ads and are subdued in design, which some will find appropriate for a literary magazine. An ad provided by a business may require special camera work to reproduce; check with your printer. Be sure you make clear to advertisers what their ads will look like. If you are designing ads for businesses, show them samples of how the ads will look or approve the ads with them before printing.

Patronships

Unlike an ad, you are not selling patrons a practical service; you are asking them to make an investment in the arts. Sports teams often solicit patrons. If you sell patronships, you represent your staff as an arts organization with carefully thought out goals. Show potential patrons your goals (see Chapter 1). Patrons who feel your goals are valuable ones will be willing to support your efforts with a cash donation.

> **A listing of patrons shows that the community supports you.**

Patrons are usually acknowledged with a simple listing of names (see Figure 2.6). At the symphony, the theatre, or any number of sports events, such listings will often appear in the back of the program. Patrons can be individuals, families, clubs, businesses, classes, or whoever. If space allows, provide extra lines below the names for an address or short message. The opportunity to write a creative message can become a selling point in itself. A listing of patrons shows that the community supports you, and listings can easily be accommodated in any literary magazine, regardless of format or printing method.

Offer patrons a free copy of your new issue. If they care enough about your cause to support it, they will want to see the results. To make a profit, be sure that the price of a patronship is more than the actual cost, not just the cover price, of a single copy.

You may also want to create different price brackets for patrons' support. Make the lowest bracket very affordable, and its income potential may surprise you. You can develop interesting names for the price brackets. The names might relate to the title of the magazine or the current issue's design concept. Some possible bracket names include:

Figure 2.6
Magazine Spread with
Patron Listing

In addition to advertising, the
HARBINGER staff (Lakewood H.S.,
Lakewood, CO) sells patronships of two,
three, and four lines, labeled "Patrons,"
"Sponsors," and "Friends."

- Patrons, Sponsors, Friends
- Cherubs, Angels, Archangels
- Iron, Bronze, Copper, Silver, Gold
- Moons, Planets, Stars, Galaxies

Grants and Subsidies

Funds within a school may be available for the asking. Departmental
funds, subsidies from the school activities budget, grants from the
school board, monies allocated to programs for the gifted and talented,
and other funds may be available if staff members present a well-
organized package of the magazine's goals, standards, and budget
needs. There may even be a business or professional organization in
the community willing to underwrite part or all of an issue. Approach
such groups with carefully planned print materials as suggested in the
section on approaching advertisers and patrons, and be prepared to
give a sincere, concise oral summary of your situation.

Find out if your school newspaper or yearbook receives any subsidies. If they do, the same sources may be open to a literary magazine.

Donations of Services and Materials

Typesetters, desktop publishers, printers, art supply stores, and other
businesses with whom you deal to produce a magazine may be willing
to donate services or materials in exchange for advertising or other acknowledgment. Such businesses may also be willing to reduce rates for
a school publication. These people are in business to make a profit, of
course, but the business world also cares about helping education. The
best possibilities are businesspeople who have strong ties with your

Why We Don't Do Bake Sales

A literary magazine staff of ten runs a bake sale. Here is how their time was spent earning money in one week:

Ten people spent one hour debating various fund-raisers and decided to do a bake sale. (ten work-hours)

Ten people spent one-half hour organizing where and when to hold the sale, who would work the table and when, who would publicize the sale and how, who would bake, and what the prices would be. (five work-hours)

Ten people spent at least one hour baking, making posters, or helping in some other way. (ten work-hours plus all the groceries donated to the cause)

Six people spent one hour selling the baked goods. (six work-hours)

Thirty-one work-hours resulted in earning $45.00. Everyone helped, they organized efficiently, and they earned $1.45 per work-hour.

Compare the bake sale to the income from a campaign selling ads and patronships in nine weeks:

Ten people spent three hours learning about advertising and patronships and then role-playing sales situations. (30 work-hours)

Ten people spent one hour helping produce contracts, fact sheets, and other materials to present to potential advertisers and patrons. (ten work-hours)

Ten people spent five hours making phone contacts, driving, and talking with potential advertisers and patrons. (50 work-hours)

In 90 work-hours, each staff member sold a minimum of $50.00 in ads and patronships, which means they earned over $500.00 as a staff. They earned more than $5.56 per work-hour.

school, like alumni or parents. It does not hurt to ask. In asking, be prepared to make a well-organized presentation as you would to an advertiser or patron.

School Fund-Raisers

There are endless possibilities for school fund-raisers, including: having bake sales; sponsoring faculty-student competitions, movies, or dances; selling chances to guess the number of jelly beans; compiling or selling coupon books; selling candles, stationery, bleacher pads, breakfast, or products bearing the school's name; or being sponsored for whatever something-a-thon will work.

If any of these fund-raisers works well for you, use them. Many of them add to school spirit. Some of them are good sources of revenue. If a fund-raiser becomes traditional, the publicity value for a magazine can be great. Such projects offer the staff a chance to work together and learn organizational and publicity skills.

On the other hand, some fund-raisers involve financial risk, and many consume large amounts of valuable staff meeting time with organizational details. Some fund-raisers might be successful when run by a large club, but literary magazine staffs tend to be relatively small. Before engaging in a school fund-raiser, evaluate its potential fund-raising capacity per work-hour. Try not to work below minimum wage.

Selling Services

A staff that has learned the production aspects of magazine journalism, covered in Chapter 5, has a saleable skill. The school registration guide, programs for concerts and plays, and other print products on campus may currently be designed and pasted up by an off-campus printer. Offer to design and paste up these projects at a reasonable rate. School organizations, athletic teams, and community organizations may be pleased to find less expensive services and a chance to benefit a worthy cause. Such projects also give a staff production experience before tackling the magazine itself.

With pasteup and design skills, a staff can also produce its own products for sale. A book cover, for example, designed by the staff and paid for by a school booster group or ads on the back cover, could include school-related dates, study skills, poems, or anti-drug information. As with school fund-raisers, above, calculate the fund-raising potential per work-hour before tackling a project that sells the staff's skills.

CONTACTING POTENTIAL ADVERTISERS AND PATRONS

To successfully sell ads or patronships, become knowledgeable about your magazine and your student body, compile a kit of information for prospective buyers, and practice skills to make the session go well.

What to Do Beforehand

Prepare a fact sheet. Both patrons and advertisers will ask about the project in which they are investing. Prepare a fact sheet, no more than one page long, of interesting information about your magazine. Use a logo, interesting type, school letterhead, or a strong border to give it authority. The printing need not be expensive, but anything produced by a literary magazine staff should be easy to read, visually pleasant,

Possible Questions for Fact Sheet

1. How many years has the magazine been published?
2. How often and when do you publish?
3. What is the cover price?
4. How many copies are printed?
5. How many staff members are there?
6. How is the staff organized?
7. When does the staff meet? Do staff members receive academic credit or any other acknowledgment of their efforts?
8. What is the actual cost of producing a single copy of the magazine?
9. What are the magazine's sources of funding?
10. Has the magazine entered any contests or received any awards? Have any works within the magazine received awards?
11. How large is the student body the magazine serves? What ages are members of the student body?
12. How many works (art and literature) are printed in one issue?
13. How many works are produced or submitted for consideration for each issue?
14. Who decides which works will be printed? How do they decide?
15. Who does the typesetting and printing for the magazine? Who designs it and pastes it up?
16. What have students in the past said about this magazine?
17. How will this new issue be different from past issues?
18. Are there any interesting stories or trivia about the magazine?
19. Who is the magazine's advisor? How long has she been advisor? What is the advisor's work phone number? Also, leave a space for the staff member using the fact sheet to fill in his own name and phone number.

and mechanically correct. Be prepared to answer questions about information on the fact sheet. Print plenty of copies so that staff members can leave them with potential investors.

Survey the student body's spending habits. Advertisers will want to know "Will the students who read the literary magazine spend money with my business?" To answer the advertiser's question, survey the student body about their spending habits. Figure 2.7 can serve as a model for you to adapt to reflect your student body and community.

Consider joining forces to conduct this survey with the newspaper staff or some other group on campus who could also use the information. Additional help to compose, distribute, and tally the survey may be available from business, economics, computer, or math classes. Local banks and businesses may also offer assistance or have statistics about student spending available. As with the fact sheet, create a flyer for potential advertisers that summarizes the results of the survey.

Set rates for ads and patronships. How much can you charge for patronships or for ads? The answer is "what the market will bear." Various brackets for patrons were discussed under "Patronships." How much to charge for the most expensive bracket, however, will require guessing and experimentation. Ad rates will present the same problem.

Ads are sold by page portions (1/8 page ad, 1/4 page ad, and so forth) or column inches. A column inch is a space the width of a column and one inch long. In setting rates, look at the rates charged by your school's newspaper and yearbook. Examine the ways in which a literary magazine is different from, and similar to, these other two publications. A literary magazine, for example, may not print as many copies as the newspaper, but a magazine ad has a longer life, since students usually keep literary magazines. Debate how similarities and differences should affect ad rates. Check rates charged by publications at neighboring schools, too. Finally, consider asking businesses themselves what they would be willing to pay.

Figure 2.7

CCC Inkling Marketing Survey

Your answers to the following questions will help the INKLING staff maximize its advertising efforts for our next issue. Thank you for your time and effort.

1. Sex: male _____   female _____

2. Age: _____

3. Did you read the last issue of INKLING? yes no
    Did you read any of the ads? yes no

4. Did you buy a copy of the last INKLING? yes no

5. Did your parents read the last issue of INKLING? yes no

6. To start this school year, how much money did you and your parents spend on your clothes?
    under $50_____ under $100_____ under $250_____ over $250_____

7. Do you receive a monthly allowance? yes no
    If yes, how much?
    under $10_____ $10–$25_____ $26–$50_____
    over $50_____

8. Do you have a job? yes no
    If yes, how much do you earn monthly before taxes?
    under $50_____ $51–$150_____ $151–$250_____
    over $250_____

9. Name two areas or centers where you shop often:
    a. _____   b. _____

10. About how many times a month do you see movies? _____

11. Approximately how much money do you spend on food and snacks each week other than on school lunches or food at home? _____

12. Do you have a savings account? yes no

13. Do you own a car? yes no

14. How many times do you go out on a date monthly? _____

15. On a typical date, how much money do *you* spend? _____

16. Name three of your hobbies:
    a. _____   b. _____   c. _____
    About how much do you spend on your favorite hobby every month? _____

17. On which of the following items do you usually spend money every week? Circle as many as apply:
    tapes records CDs gasoline cosmetics flowers clothes
    movies dances school supplies books knick-knacks
    magazines candy ice cream pizza burgers jewelry gum
    auto supplies VCR rentals video games posters concerts
    salad bar computer supplies T-shirts nice restaurants

Prepare contracts for advertising and patronships. Staffs will need separate contracts for patrons and for advertisers. Models for each are provided in Figures 2.8 and 2.9.

Prepare goal statements. Patrons, who are investing in a literary magazine as a project of value to the staff, student body, and community, will want to know the goals of that project. Prepare a flyer to leave with potential patrons stating the staff's goals. Use the same high standards in preparing this flyer used in preparing the fact sheet, student body survey, and the contract.

Practice. Once each staff member has a packet of information, practice conducting a sales session. The skills of selling a product in which you genuinely believe will help you in any profession. You may not think of yourself as a salesperson. Still, with practice you can raise money.

Talking with Advertisers and Patrons

Dress appropriately for sales appointments; see yourself through the eyes of the businessperson you are about to visit. Staff members might consider teaming up to make calls. Two can be more effective than one.

Figure 2.8

Hardrock University STRATA Patron's Contract

STRATA is our literary magazine. It receives only partial support from the university. Help us reach our goal of distributing STRATA free to every student on campus.

Donation: $ _____
(28 spaces maximum per line—PLEASE PRINT LEGIBLY)
PATRON: $5.00

_____ (name)

FRIEND: $15.00

_____ (name)
_____ (address or message)

DONOR: $25.00 or more

_____ (name)
_____ (address)
_____ (slogan or message)

_____   _____
        Date   Patron's name or business name

_____   _____
   Patron's signature   Patron's address
(Return top to staff member)   Phone: _____

– –

PATRON'S RECEIPT   Date_____
Donation: $_____ to the Hardrock University STRATA.

_____   _____
   Patron's name   Staff member's signature

Thank you for supporting literature at HU. All patrons will receive a free copy of STRATA in March. Further questions may be addressed to Jacob Gold, Advisor, 771-0344.

Figure 2.9

South High School GATHERING PLACE
a literary-art magazine
Advertising Contract for Volume 12, February 1993

Rate: $40 per ⅛ page, minus $5 per additional eighth purchased

_____ If you are sending artwork *with* this contract, please check the line to the left. We must pick up all artwork by January 15th.

_____ If you would like the staff of GATHERING PLACE to design an ad for you, check the line to the left. A staff artist will contact you for details.

_____ Do you have a preference for the position of your ad in our magazine? If so, please check the line to the left. A staff member will contact you in January so that you may choose a particular space.

Date _____

Ad Space Purchased:

⅛ page   ¼ page   ⅜ page   ½ page   full page

Amount Received: $_____

Business's name _____

Address _____ Phone _____

Signature of Advertiser _____

Salesperson for GATHERING PLACE _____

One copy to advertiser/one copy to GATHERING PLACE

   Advertisers will receive a free copy of GATHERING PLACE in February. Thank you for your support. Michelle Vigil, Advisor, 324-1882.

Here are some steps to follow in conducting a sales session. You can adapt them to fit your circumstances and style. The basic presentation should take about ten minutes.

First, find out who to talk to and, if necessary, make an appointment. Take to your appointment copies of all the handouts the staff prepared. Put them in a folder of some sort that looks nice. Also, take copies of your magazine's last issue. At the meeting, begin by introducing yourself. Tell your first and last name, the school you are from, and the magazine you represent. Include your position on the staff. Do not rush.

Next, state that you would like to talk about: (1) the possibility of her advertising in your magazine, or (2) the possibility of her support as a patron. Then, show your listener the magazine. Show the cover, being sure that it is in a position from which she can see it easily. Then, flip through the magazine, stopping at three or four works to comment about them. Be sure to show ads or patronships. Practice handling the magazine beforehand. If at any point she wants to take the magazine from you, offer it to her.

Throughout the meeting, invite interaction. Do not head into a set routine and numb the listener into silence. Pause often. You are in a stronger position if the conversation is interactive, not one-way.

Next, move to the survey of student spending, for advertisers, or the goals statement, for patrons. State what the handout is about, hand it

Show your listener the magazine.

to her, and point out two or three significant items on it. Then offer her the fact sheet, many points of which you may already have covered. If you had no back issue to show, you will have more time to spend on handouts. Finally, bring out the contract and ask her if she would like an ad or patronship. In leaving, with or without a signed contract, thank her for her time. Ask her if she would like to keep the magazine, if you can spare it. Leave her all the handouts.

There may be several reasons to check back with an advertiser or patron. If you need to pick up a check or artwork, or to meet again with someone who still needs to think about his decision, arrange a specific time and day before leaving your first meeting. If, after seeing a person twice, he still has not committed himself, you probably do not have a sale. Spend your time on other possibilities.

Create a system for the staff to list contacts they have made. Be sure to check it before arranging appointments so as not to waste time covering the same ground. Also, any paid advertiser or patron who is accidentally contacted again by another staff member will feel the staff is not well organized or appreciative of her purchase.

Questions and Activities

1. What sources of funding are not discussed in this section and should be considered by your literary magazine?
2. List all the different sources of funding you think your literary magazine should pursue.
3. Given the information available to the staff at this point, what do you feel is a reasonable cover price for your magazine?
4. Working in groups of three, choose a fund-raising event with which one of you has been involved. Calculate, as nearly as possible, the fund-raising potential per work-hour for that event.
5. How comfortable do you feel in the role of salesperson? Do you feel more comfortable selling to the student body or to the business community? Does your comfort level depend on whether you are selling an ad, patronship, baked goods, candles, or the magazine itself? Explain your answers.
6. Suggest two specific ideas to make a visually pleasant fact sheet, ad contract, or other handout for your magazine.
7. How would you change the sales session outlined in this section to fit your personal style and circumstances? Practice your sales technique by role-playing a sales session.

SELLING THE MAGAZINE

Nothing is quite like the sensation of selling something you created yourself. It is like lighting candles in the dark or launching a fleet of boats. Finding out that other people are excited about what you are excited about is wonderful. Still, that excitement does not come out of nowhere; you must launch a good campaign.

LAUNCHING A GOOD CAMPAIGN

All the characteristics outlined in "Launching a Good Campaign" and "Posters and Showcases" are also characteristics of a good magazine sales campaign. With experience campaigning for submissions and soliciting funds, you will be well-tuned for a campaign to sell a literary magazine. You will need to overcome the fatigue involved in making final deadlines to carefully organize a good sales campaign. After all, all your effort in producing the magazine amounts to very little if no one sees the results.

Setting the Cover Price

The price often does not appear on the cover of a scholastic literary magazine. This allows the staff time to balance the success of fund-raising, the printer's bill, and other factors. The printer's bill, particularly, often cannot be determined exactly until the printer sees the actual pages he is to print and calculates the costs involved on each one. A professional typesetter's bill may have similar variances.

Presales

Selling copies before the magazine is even printed may help generate anticipation of the magazine's arrival, help predict how many copies can be sold, and help raise funds early in production to purchase supplies and services. If the fees payment system on your campus allows for prepaying at the beginning of the term for athletic fees, art fees, and the yearbook, then it may be possible to arrange with the school bookkeeper a prepayment for the literary magazine. The cost of a literary magazine will seem quite reasonable compared to many other fees. If the literary magazine cannot be added to regular fees, set up your own presales through English classes or at a sales table. Since the price may be difficult to determine so early in the production schedule, set a reasonably low presale price. If the actual price is higher, readers who have supported you through presales will benefit.

SELLING TO THE STUDENT BODY

Relative to the literary magazine, the student body will divide itself into three categories:

- Students who definitely will buy the magazine
- Students who might buy the magazine
- Students who definitely will not buy the magazine

You may be able to determine the relative size of each category through a student survey.

A campaign for students who will definitely buy the magazine needs to use a variety of methods to be sure students know where to buy the magazine and how much it costs. After that, the magazine will sell itself to this group because it is something they want: a collection of works by their peers.

There are students who definitely will not buy a literary magazine, any literary magazine. The only campaign that will reach this group is one that distributes the magazine free to the entire student body, which is something you may want to do, funding your magazine through alternative sources. Consider, too, asking the English or art departments to buy a set for classroom use. This way, your magazine will be in the hands of some students who definitely will not buy a literary magazine.

Students who *might* buy the magazine present a real challenge. They are not totally turned off by the idea of a literary magazine, but they need more than knowing where to get one and glimpsing an interesting cover to convince them to make a purchase. Good one-to-one sales technique can be effective. A staff member who speaks enthusiastically and warmly about his magazine can convince someone to buy and read it.

A sales campaign with an "image" can be effective. A combination of posters, announcements, and sales tables can promote your magazine's image, for example, as something to have because it is "cool," or because it is an important memory of the school year, or because it is "radical" and "outrageous."

Gimmicks and special offers can be effective, but choose carefully. Know your student body and pick an idea that will be viewed as creative and new, not as a desperate last effort. You might create a package for buying the yearbook and literary magazine together. Arrange a deal for a free movie or pizza with the purchase of a magazine. Arrange for a discount at a local bookstore. Put together a poetry reading of works from your magazine and other works, combining purchase of the magazine with the ticket price.

> **Promote your magazine's image as something to have because it is "cool," or because it is an important memory of the school year, or because it is "radical" and "outrageous."**

SELLING TO THE COMMUNITY

What is happening in education concerns citizens in your community. Beyond the parents and friends of your school who want to read your magazine, there are people who would like to know what students think. A literary magazine is a good source of answers. Selling door-to-door in your neighborhood may work. Consider selling copies of your magazine to any business that has a reception room with magazines, like doctors or car dealerships. Consider putting together a box holding a dozen copies and displaying it on the counters of drugstores, bookstores, and other businesses close to your campus. These and other sales strategies you devise can widen your reading audience.

Bookstores often feature works by local authors and artists. A bookstore display is an excellent opportunity to sell your literary magazine to the community.

Questions and Activities

1. A good sales campaign is multidimensional, using a variety of methods to contact the target audience. List three specific methods you would use to make sure the student body knows where to buy a literary magazine and for how much.

2. What are four factors you should consider in finalizing your cover price?

3. What two strategies should your magazine staff use to persuade students who might buy a magazine to actually buy one?

4. Should your staff plan to sell magazines to the community? If so, what two strategies would you suggest?

5. Practice your one-to-one sales technique by role-playing a magazine sale with other staff members.

CHAPTER THREE

CRITIQUING MANUSCRIPTS

GETTING UNDERWAY

The soul of any literary magazine is, of course, its contents. This is probably what you have been waiting to get to since the first day the staff met. This chapter deals with handling manuscripts. Some reference is made to artworks, too, wherever artworks and literature have shared concerns. Artworks for the most part, however, are dealt with in Chapter 4, "Designing the Magazine." Much of Chapter 3's contents you will need right away, because you will probably have manuscripts to handle as soon as publicity gets out to students. Part of your staff may even want to begin work on Chapter 3 at the same time that other staff members are organizing publicity.

Some of Chapter 3, though, you will need to study during the design and layout stage of production. Proofing manuscripts for errors, for example, will be something you do now, as you handle accepted manuscripts, and something you do later, when final copies are being readied for the printer. Both stages of proofing are covered in this chapter.

STRATEGIES FOR CHOOSING MANUSCRIPTS

Like it or not, a literary magazine staff must accept some manuscripts and reject others. Often a magazine staff simply receives or writes more submissions than it can print. Even if a staff received just the right number of manuscripts to fill a magazine, the staff would probably make decisions that some were not of the quality needed, others not suited for their reading audience. All of them together might not combine in a pleasing balance of genres and subjects.

Chapter 3 examines the process of critiquing manuscripts: from debating a work's literary quality, to its audience appeal, to its legal implications. To critique a manuscript, then, is to judge its merits. This section begins by suggesting four strategies for choosing manuscripts. Adapt or combine these strategies to find a workable one for your staff.

TAKE EACH AUTHOR'S BEST

Consider setting a maximum and minimum number of works in a batch.

For this strategy, the staff asks authors to submit a batch of works. The staff then chooses the best one or two works of each batch, depending on length and quality. The publicity campaign must make clear that authors who submit works according to the staff's instructions will have something printed.

In using this strategy, consider setting a maximum and minimum number of works in a batch. Without a maximum number, some authors might submit entire journals; without a minimum number, other authors might submit a single work, which the staff would be obligated to print.

This strategy demands space to accommodate many authors. The quality of works chosen will vary widely. Be prepared to limit artwork, since the number of pages demanded may consume much of your

There are many talented writers in your campus and community. Encourage those individuals to submit works to your magazine.

budget. As a result, be prepared to find interesting ways to break up the large blocks of uninterrupted text that this strategy may generate.

When this strategy works, the student body sees their magazine as a forum for their peer group and a smorgasbord of reading choices.

START A CREATIVE WRITING CLUB

A staff might choose to work directly with authors as they write, rather than soliciting finished works. In this case, the staff becomes the core and leadership of a larger group that meets regularly to read, review, critique, rewrite, and revise manuscripts. Such groups are often called creative writing clubs. The staff takes responsibility for organizing and publicizing meetings as well as producing the magazine itself.

In a creative writing club, writers bring works in progress to meetings for suggestions. Suggestions would come from staff members, who would probably also be writers sharing their works, and from other non-staff writers attending meetings. In fact, such a club might begin as a group of writers and gradually evolve a literary magazine staff from its ranks. In either case, the meetings become forums for discussing works in progress, coaching writers on style, structure, and content. If the process is successful, each writer who attends meetings regularly and responds to suggestions for improvement should be represented in the magazine.

When this strategy works, the students see the magazine as a polished product of a committed group of writers representing excellence in the student body.

USE A PANEL OF JUDGES

The staff might decide to have a panel of judges choose the manuscripts to be printed. The panel, presumably experts in analysis of literature, might be retired faculty members, college professors, alumni, journalists, or authors.

Using a panel of judges, particularly a panel of experts from outside your school, can relieve the pressure on the staff of being the experts. Sometimes involving a panel of experts can boost interest in creative writing. An outside panel also makes possible the objective awarding of prizes. Particularly if staff members' works are included in the judging, a panel may be necessary so that the staff does not act as both contestants and judges. Students may view being chosen for the magazine as a significant honor in itself.

Because a judge's time is valuable and probably volunteered, carefully prepare all manuscripts for easy handling, being sure they are readable and carefully numbered. Attach to each any necessary evaluation forms. If several hundred works are submitted, the staff may need to narrow the possibilities to a reasonable number of manuscripts for judges to read in the time available.

When this strategy works, the student body views their magazine as a special collection validated by respected critics.

> **An outside panel makes possible the objective awarding of prizes.**

SOLICIT FOR OPEN SUBMISSIONS

Soliciting for open submissions means that the staff launches a publicity campaign encouraging the student body to submit works, and the staff then chooses the best of those works. This is the simplest of the strategies outlined. In fact, all the strategies outlined above are to some degree variations on this basic idea.

The success of open submissions depends on students confident enough as creative writers to submit their works. More than any other strategy, success also depends on the student body's trust in the staff. Therefore, in using this strategy, be clear and open about the critiquing procedures used and assure fairness in every way possible.

Unlike the "Take Each Author's Best" strategy, many authors will be turned away, but the quality of the literature should be more consistent. Unlike a creative writing club, a good campaign for open submissions can draw in submissions from talented writers who, for whatever reason, would never join a writing club. Unlike using a panel of judges, the power of choice remains with students.

When this strategy works, the student body sees their magazine as a showcase of excellence and diversity.

Questions and Activities

1. List one advantage and one disadvantage for each of the four given strategies for accepting manuscripts.
2. What strategy or strategies should your magazine use for accepting manuscripts? Why?
3. Are there ways in which your staff would need to alter a strategy to make it workable for your school?

MANAGING MANUSCRIPT FILES

> A staff that runs a successful campaign soliciting for manuscripts risks drowning in a sea of paper.

A staff that runs a successful campaign soliciting for manuscripts risks drowning in a sea of paper. With dozens of manuscripts to handle—some accepted, some rejected, some to be revised, some proofed, some being illustrated—your staff will need an efficient system for filing manuscripts. A staff member should know when he picks up a manuscript what has or has not been done with it. If he cannot tell, the entire staff risks miscommunication and loss of time. This section outlines ideas for systematic handling of manuscript files.

TAG ALONG

As manuscripts arrive for consideration by the staff, tag each one. Tagged manuscripts are easier to file and to handle in all stages of magazine production. To tag a manuscript, first give it a number, numbering consecutively (1, 2, 3 . . .). If several short works have been submitted on a single sheet of paper, separate them, and give each work a separate number. If you are going to print the best of each author's works, you will need to know which works are by the same author, so give all works by the same author the same number and use letters to identify individual works (14a, 14b, 14c . . .).

Tagging manuscripts has the advantage of not revealing which works are by the same author. Another advantage is that manuscripts with numbers are easier to handle. There is never any doubt which work is being referred to. Reading assignments are easy to give: "Read through number 30 by tomorrow." Details like checking manuscripts out to a typesetter are easy when all the editor has to do is write down manuscript numbers.

After tagging each manuscript with its number, record basic information about it in the staff's manuscript log book (see Figure 3.1). Needless to say, guard this book very carefully. As a complete record of all manuscripts submitted, your log is very valuable and will have many uses.

As each manuscript is carefully tagged and recorded in the log book, obliterate the author's name wherever it appears on the manuscript. (The only staff which would achieve no advantage by removing names would be a staff working with a creative writing club.) Manuscripts with numbers can be handled more fairly in the critiquing process than manuscripts with names. The names of friends or enemies and the sex or ethnic background of students cannot bias the staff's evaluation if it does not see the names.

Figure 3.1

LJHS HERITAGE Manuscript Log		
MS#	AUTHOR	TITLE or FIRST LINE
1	Bill Swanson	"The Inquiry"
2	Bill Swanson	"Seventh Sense of a Sailor"
3	Brigitte Salas	"It wasn't a dark and stormy night..."
4	Mountain Brightstar	"Word Perfect"
5	Anna Green	"Tuba or Not Tuba"

In your publicity campaign, make known that works are critiqued without name and by number; students will appreciate your fairness. After critiquing, of course, authors' names must be restored to accepted manuscripts, but the number will stay with the manuscript and be useful throughout your magazine's production.

Trust the tagging of manuscripts to one incredibly reliable person. This person may need one incredibly reliable assistant in case of illness or when many manuscripts need tagging. Ideally, if your staff organization makes it possible, the manuscript tagger should be someone who is not critiquing manuscripts.

ROUTING MANUSCRIPTS

"Has this poem been critiqued yet?"
"Has number 42 been proofed?"
"Where do I put this play when I've typed it?"
"Is this one supposed to be revised?"

When staff members ask these sorts of questions, they need an organized filing system. Before these questions even start to come up, organize a file system that reflects the decisions your staff has made about how manuscripts will be handled. Organize this system as quickly as possible, because once the staff gets involved in critiquing, it will become easy to allow manuscripts to stack up, ignoring the next step in manuscript handling.

Study the sample routing system in Figure 3.2. In this system, most numbers represent a numbered file folder. Inside each file folder is an outline of what task needs to be done at that stage and which folder a manuscript goes to next.

Notice that the sample routing system differentiates between a typed manuscript and a typeset manuscript. A typed manuscript is one produced on a typewriter or with a word processor; a staff may handle typed manuscripts throughout production. A typeset manuscript is one ready for the printer's camera. From typeset, the actual printing plates will be made. Details about typesetting and other functions mentioned in Steps 9 through 15 in Figure 3.2 are covered in Chapter 5 under "Turning Out Typeset," page 119–25.

For the sake of efficiency and security of the manuscripts, manuscripts should not leave the staff room. A manuscript buried in someone's notebook, tossed on the kitchen table, or left next to a typewriter is out of the system. It cannot be accepted, rejected, revised, proofed, discussed, placed, assigned, illustrated, or returned to the author. If needed, photocopy or type extra copies of manuscripts for illustrators or layout teams, being sure to mark such copies as duplicates. If your system demands that manuscripts must leave the staff room for any reason, organize a checkout system.

TYING IT DOWN

As a final check for efficiency and security of the manuscripts, staple a routing sheet to each accepted manuscript. As a quality control, a routing sheet can confirm who did what to the manuscript. Also, a manu-

Figure 3.2
Manuscript Routing System

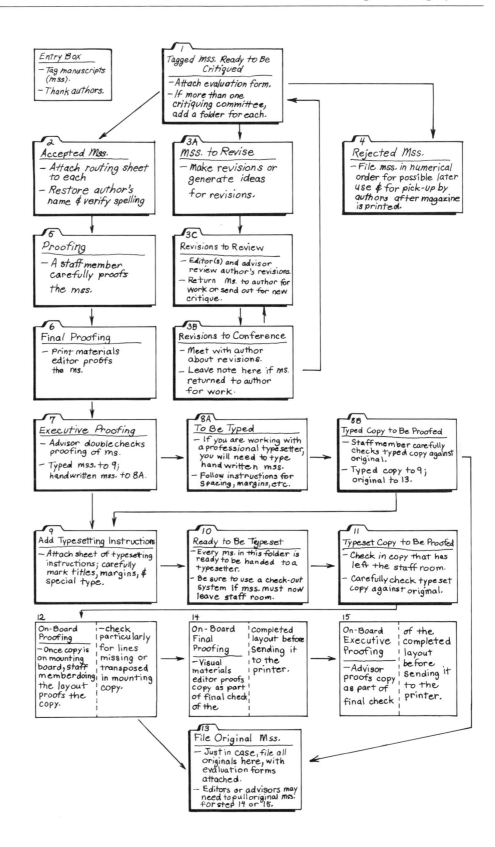

Figure 3.3

DJC ARTIFACT Routing Sheet

As you process each manuscript, initial in the appropriate blank the task you have completed and route the manuscript to the appropriate folder. This form should be stapled to the top of every manuscript accepted or to be revised.

Manuscript Number: _____

Author's name (write clearly) _____

_____ Correct spelling of author's name confirmed (2)

_____ Revisions recommended by critiquing committee

      _____ Suggested revisions attached (3A)

      _____ Revisions made by author (3B)

      _____ Revisions reviewed by editor (3C)

_____ Original proofed—staff member (5)

_____ Original proofed—editor (6)

_____ Original proofed—advisor (7)

      Typing for typesetter

      _____ Copy typed (8A)

      _____ Typed copy proofed (8B)

_____ Instructions to typesetter completed (9)

_____ Copy typeset (10)

_____ Typeset copy proofed (11)

For final on-board proofing, staff members will initial the mounting board itself.

  Manuscript assigned to page _____

  Layout assigned to _____

  Illustration assigned to _____

script accidentally left lying around can be quickly tied back into the system, because the routing sheet clearly identifies what has been handled. Figure 3.3 shows a sample routing sheet that you may adapt to your staff's needs. The numbers in parentheses correspond to the folder numbers in Figure 3.2.

Questions and Activities

1. What are two advantages to tagging manuscripts?
2. Are there terms in the sample routing sheet that you do not know? If so, look them up in the Glossary.
3. How might a routing sheet for your magazine differ from the sample given in this section?
4. Draw a diagram showing a manuscript routing system that will work for your magazine. Number the stages and outline what task will happen at each stage.

READING MANUSCRIPTS

It is the staff's task to evaluate manuscripts fairly, whether to choose the best ones for publication, to suggest improvements for revision, or to screen the manuscripts for a panel of judges. The atmosphere the staff establishes for reading is important so that successful critiquing follows.

Each staff member involved in the critiquing process should read manuscripts before attending sessions to critique them. This reading should be done individually and quietly, avoiding the distractions of other staff members and friends. Make folders of manuscripts available in the staff room, so that each person can report there to read during free time. If a few staff members report to read at the same time, at least the group will be small and the established atmosphere will be one of quiet concentration. A process like this encourages each staff member to form a fresh, independent judgment, unswayed by group opinion. This is what is fair to the author.

Staff members reading in groups will be tempted to comment as manuscripts are passed from one to another. It is difficult for people who love literature not to comment, positively or negatively, as they experience new works. Imagine trying to form an independent opinion about a manuscript passed to you with a grin and "Wait'll you read this one." Imagine someone across the room muttering, "Sure isn't much to read this week" or "Junk." You may consider yourself a strong personality, independent and unlikely to be swayed by such off-hand comments, but they do have an effect. Debate the merits of manuscripts only after staff members have read them independently and formed their own initial opinions.

Imagine trying to form an independent opinion about a manuscript passed to you with a grin and "Wait'll you read this one."

Staff members should read manuscripts carefully and keep notes about what they have read. Attentive reading ensures a fair critiquing process.

WHEN TO READ MANUSCRIPTS ALOUD— AND WHEN NOT TO

Creative writing is wonderful to read aloud, so why not read each manuscript aloud to the group and then critique it? Such a technique may sound appealing, but the critique that follows an oral reading may be as much a critique of the performance as of the manuscript itself. A metered poem read without awareness of its meter may appear to han-

Why not read each manuscript aloud to the group and then critique it?

dle rhythm poorly. A story read in a monotone may seem monotonous. An essay read with deep feeling may appear to contain more feeling than the author wrote. Such a technique also leaves out the visual appearance of the work on the page, a particularly important aspect of poetry. An oral reading would not allow the listeners to see that a poem is an acrostic.

Good Times to Read Manuscripts Aloud

- To celebrate. Once a work has been chosen, the act of reading it to the whole staff can celebrate your magazine as it comes into being. Reading accepted works can also stimulate discussion about illustration and placement of the work.
- To persuade. In the process of debating the merits of a work, read parts of it aloud. The act of reading can help others hear and see the work the way you do.
- To understand. As you read a work for the first time, such elements as its purpose, dialogue, rhythms, and tone may be challenging. Reading aloud may offer a different perspective.

KEEPING A RECORD

Several days may pass before the manuscripts you read last come up in a critiquing session. Critiquing sessions will bog down if the discussion of each manuscript begins with "Which one is that? I don't remember it very well." Figure 3.4 shows a simple form that allows staff members to keep a record of how far they have read and how they reacted to each work. Critiquing sessions will run more smoothly when staff members use a form like this consistently, making notes as they read and bringing those notes to critiquing sessions. These notes need be comprehensible only to the person who wrote them. For obvious reasons, notes should not be written directly on the manuscript itself or on any form attached to the manuscript.

WHY DON'T WE READ THEM ALL FIRST, THEN DECIDE?

Wouldn't it be best if the staff read all the manuscripts to be considered first, then decided which ones to print? The answer to this question might be "yes" if the total number of manuscripts your staff reviews is small and if your production schedule allows sufficient time after the submissions deadline for evaluation of all works and production of the magazine.

An advantage to the reading-then-deciding method is that the staff can gain a perspective by seeing everything that is available before deciding. The staff will know how many love poems, essays, plays, science fiction works, and so forth are available and can easily make choices to balance the range of subjects and genres in the magazine. Additionally, staff members will find it easier to set standards for acceptance when all the manuscripts are in front of them at one time.

Figure 3.4

	UC BALLAST Reading Log
Ms. Number	**Comments**
12	??- Confusing! Supposed to be funny? Help! Symbolic of arms race?
13	1-act, characters complex, symbols good. Teen/parent theme typical.
(14)	WOW! Yes!! (nonfiction)-onomatopoeia (traffic noises)
15	Good opening, ending fizzles - breaks own rhyme pattern in last stanza
16	Sunset poem - clichés

Finally, debate over some borderline manuscripts may take less time when staff members see what they have that might be better to print.

A disadvantage to reading-then-deciding is that this process delays most work on the production of the magazine until well past the submissions deadline. Also, reading-then-deciding tends to encourage a staff to see works in comparative terms, so that critiquing centers around which work is better, rather than looking at the specific qualities within each work. Such critiquing can become a debate of personal preferences. Comparative critiquing can also lead to awkward comparisons of works that are of drastically different genres, forms, and moods.

The alternative to reading-then-deciding is deciding-as-you-read. Deciding-as-you-read means that the staff begins reading and critiquing manuscripts as soon as they begin accumulating in the submissions box.

An advantage of deciding-as-you-read is that this process extends the available time for production of the magazine. An illustration, for example, will be better the more time is available to locate or produce art that really interacts well with a piece of literature. Another advantage to this process is that critiquing tends to focus on the individual merits of each work, rather than on comparisons with other works.

A disadvantage of deciding-as-you-read is that it is sometimes hard to establish minimum standards for acceptance. This might be particularly true for a magazine in its first year, not knowing what to expect in terms of the quantity or quality of the submissions. Another disadvantage of deciding-as-you-read is that it is sometimes harder to balance the magazine, since the staff may not be able to anticipate what genres or subjects will appear often in submissions.

1. When and where will your staff read manuscripts before critiquing them?
2. What are three good reasons for reading a manuscript aloud?
3. How might a reading log for your magazine differ from the sample given in this section?
4. Which process should your magazine use: reading-then-deciding or deciding-as-you-read? Why?

EVALUATION FORMS FOR CRITIQUING MANUSCRIPTS

> "Well, do we print this one or not?"

Your staff has picked a strategy for choosing manuscripts, has devised a system for managing manuscript files, and has begun to read manuscripts. Now, at last, it is time to begin debating the merits of those manuscripts.

Now your staff needs some sort of evaluation form to guide the discussion of each manuscript. It is possible, of course, to sit down as a group and simply ask each other, "Well, do we print this one or not?" Working with an evaluation form, though, will direct the group's discussion and, in fairness to every author, assure that certain important points are discussed about each manuscript.

Your next challenge is to decide what those important points are. What should be examined carefully about each manuscript? What are the deciding factors to which the critiquing committee can point and say, "Here is the reason this work deserves publication," or "Based on these weaknesses, let's suggest the author work on it and resubmit a revised version"?

IMPORTANT POINTS

For literary magazines, the important points in evaluating manuscripts should reflect objective criteria that evaluate the content, craft, style, creativity, and total impact of the work.

Content, in literature, describes the subject or topic about which the author has written, his focus and purpose in writing about the subject, and what he has to say about that subject.

Craft involves the techniques the author has used to convey his content, including structure and word choice. Ultimately, in great literature, craft and content become one: how you say it is what you say.

Style is the fingerprint on the work of the individual author, her culture, and her time period. An extension of the content and craft, style is what allows you as a reader to say, "This passage sounds like Maya Angelou."

> In a successful literary work, the total impact is more than the sum of the parts.

Creativity is the unique spark that gives life to a work. It is entirely possible to read a work with significant content and careful control of craft that fails to stimulate your imagination. The choices the author has made are simply too typical of choices many authors have made. Such a work may not have a strong sense of style, either.

The *total impact* of a work results from the interaction of content, craft, style, and creativity. A work's total impact is its ability to make the reader feel, imagine, and think deeply. In a successful literary

A well-organized filing system helps your staff track manuscripts throughout the critiquing process.

work, the total impact is more than the sum of the parts. Some works manage to have significant impact despite weakness in one area; some have little impact because of a weakness in one area.

How do you as a staff member prepare to evaluate literature in these five areas? As a person interested in literature, you have come to the staff with previous experiences preparing you to critique literature using objective literary criteria. You have studied literature in English classes and may have tried writing creatively yourself. You have read on your own, seen movies and plays, looked at art, gone to concerts, perhaps studied a second language, and had any number of experiences that have tuned your mind and senses to quality in a creative work. You will have a gut-level reaction to many of the manuscripts you read, feeling instantly whether it is a work with promise or not. The problem is, not everyone who reads a work will have the same reaction you do.

The difference in individual reactions is what starts debate. The debate, if productive, will sort out reactions resulting from personal preferences from reactions resulting from the quality of the work itself. As a good critic, you should avoid judging by criteria such as whether you like or dislike the subject, whether you like narrative poems as a genre, whether fantasy literature is something you normally read, or whether you agree with the author's viewpoint or conclusions.

Your staff must decide the depth to which you need to debate the content, craft, style, creativity, and total impact of works. Discuss as a staff your background and readiness to critique literature. You should decide what literary terms the staff should master to conduct that debate. Look through the Glossary of this textbook and discuss how many of the terms you already know and which ones you should know. Consider asking a faculty member to conduct a review lesson for the staff.

Figures 3.5 to 3.7 are samples of evaluation forms to adapt to your needs. You will notice that the third form, for one-act plays and short stories, offers a different format than the other two. It marries content and craft by addressing each of the elements of fiction. You have probably learned the elements of fiction (character, plot, setting, style, and theme) in English classes. A critiquing committee using this form would address both quality of content and quality of craft within each element.

Using a Point System

You will also notice that all three forms base debate on a 40-point system using 32 as the minimum total for acceptance. You may or may not want to include a point system on your rating form. The advantages, though, are worth considering. Works with high point totals, for example, can easily be identified as your best works so that they can be given prominent placement and illustration. Point totals may also be used to determine prizes and awards.

If the staff is working with a creative writing club, point totals can offer the author concrete feedback and a goal to achieve. A work receiving, for example, a 30 in its first critique is one the author knows is almost accepted. She knows she needs to work for two more points, and the breakdown of points by area will tell her in what areas she needs to work.

Point totals can also help you decide the final number of manuscripts to print. If the magazine is not full enough, consider pulling manuscripts with 31s from the rejected manuscript file to fill out

> **Point totals can help you decide the final number of manuscripts to print.**

Figure 3.5

JHS BALANCING ACT
Poetry Critique Form

40-point system (32 minimum to be accepted)   MS#_____

Originality and Creativity (0–10)   _____

Development of Content (0–10)   _____

   Has the author chosen a focus and poetic form appropriate to the subject? Does the work have a significant purpose and theme? Is the subject developed in an interesting way?

Craft (0–10)   _____

   Does the poem develop figurative language, mood, sensory appeal, sound elements, and other poetic devices in ways appropriate to the subject?

Style (0–5)   _____

   Does the author control sentence length, vocabulary, descriptive details, action, and word order in a way that creates a unique voice for this particular author?

Total Impact (0–5)   _____

                                    Total   _____

   Reason: Extra Pts. (0–3)   _____

                                    Grand Total   _____

Figure 3.6

JHS BALANCING ACT
Prose Critique Form

(essay, narrative, and experimental forms)

40-point system (32 minimum to be accepted)   MS#_____

Originality and Creativity (0–10)   _____

Development of Content (0–10)   _____

    Has the author chosen a focus and structure appropriate to the subject? Does the work have a significant purpose, depth, and theme/thesis? Is the subject developed in an interesting way?

Craft (0–10)   _____

    Does the work develop pace, mood, descriptive language, supporting details, figurative language, use of dialogue or quotes, and other devices in ways appropriate to the subject and genre?

Style (0–5)   _____

    Does the author control sentence length, vocabulary, descriptive details, action, and word order in a way that creates a unique voice for this particular author?

Total Impact (0–5)   _____

                   Total   _____

Reason: Extra Pts. (0–3)   _____

                  Grand Total   _____

pages. If the magazine begins to look too full, consider dropping some manuscripts with 32s or even 33s.

Finally, for any staff not working with a creative writing club, evaluation forms with point totals give your staff a concrete answer for authors who want to know why their works were not accepted. After your magazine is distributed, you will want to return manuscripts to those authors who ask for them. Consider returning them with the evaluation forms attached so that authors can see exactly how their manuscripts were scored. Be sure that no comments have been added that you would not want the author to see. Authors who see your process as fair and helpful will be more likely to support your magazine.

Scoring Extra Points

Each of the sample critiquing forms provides a space for an idea called "extra points." This category allows the critiquing committee to give one, two, or three points to a manuscript that offers something not directly dealt with by the criteria given. Extra points might be scored for humor, unusual subject matter, or a work that lends itself particularly well to illustration. You may think of other good reasons for extra points. Notice that each form asks the committee to record the reason for extra points in a space provided. Extra points can make the difference between accepting and rejecting a manuscript.

An alternative to scoring points would be to have the staff mark each area with a simple "yes," indicating that the work meets minimum requirements for acceptance in that area, or "no," the work does not meet minimum requirements. A work receiving more "yes"s than "no"s would be accepted.

Figure 3.7

JHS BALANCING ACT
Short Story and One-Act Play Critique Form

40-point system (32 minimum to be accepted)   MS#_____

Originality and Creativity (0–5)   _____

Setting (0–5)   _____

   Has the author developed the setting(s) of the story (both time and place) in appropriate detail?

Plot Development (0–5)   _____

   Has the author captured the reader's attention in the exposition, developed an interesting conflict, brought events to a logical climax, and resolved the conflict in an appropriate way?

Characterization (0–5)   _____

   Are characters interesting, distinctive as speakers, and appropriately developed?

Theme (0–5)   _____

   Does the work have a significant purpose, depth, and theme?

Language (0–5)   _____

   Has the author focused description, created an appropriate mood, and otherwise used the power of language to add to the work?

Style (0–5)   _____

   Does the author control sentence length, vocabulary, descriptive details, action, and word order in a way that creates a unique voice for this particular author?

Total Impact (0–5)   _____

	Total	_____
Reason:	Extra Pts. (0–3)	_____
	Grand Total	_____

Testing Evaluation Forms

Once your staff has chosen critiquing forms to use, test their workability by critiquing a test batch of manuscripts with the new forms. You might use the sample manuscripts in Appendix A. Be prepared to make modifications to your forms after testing them. The test batch manuscripts can, in addition to testing workability, help the staff get a feel for the breaking point between accepted and rejected manuscripts.

Questions and Activities

1. What five areas for manuscript evaluation are outlined in this section? Are there any other areas that you think should be considered?
2. What experiences have you had that prepare you to evaluate quality in a creative work?
3. Find in the Glossary six terms that you feel the staff should know before critiquing manuscripts. Why is each of these terms helpful?

4. Draft a sample critiquing form for a genre of literature that your staff is likely to handle. Be prepared to explain the advantages your form would have in the critiquing process.

HOW TO DEBATE CONSTRUCTIVELY

A staff's organizational plan may delegate the critiquing of manuscripts to a critiquing committee or to an entire staff. Whatever your staff's organizational plan, the process of critiquing manuscripts should be a group activity. A process in which staff members read manuscripts individually and then meet together to debate the merits of manuscripts will insure fair handling of every author's work. This section outlines basic procedures for groups to follow when a committee or staff meets to critique manuscripts.

BASIC PROCEDURES

The group is ready to critique. The first manuscript is in the middle of the table; everyone has a copy of the appropriate evaluation form. Here are the steps your group might take. Customize and adapt them to meet the needs of your group, being sure that your method is fair to the views of all group members and fair to each author.

First, let everyone voice the feelings and reactions the work stimulated, like "I wrote 'Confusing' in my log," "I had a lot of trouble even getting through it," "I like the use of description," "The dialogue is great," "It reminds me of other works we've read," or "It certainly is unusual." Avoid judgments of the quality of the whole work, like "It's the best thing we've read," "Boring," or "Honestly, I just hated it." These kinds of statements charge the air with confrontation but do not say anything specific to help understand the work.

Initial reactions should be voiced without challenge. The group should understand that these are first reactions, not challenges to debate. No staff member should feel angry about strongly different reactions. No staff member should feel a first reaction will be "held against" him should he change his mind; as Ralph Waldo Emerson said, "A foolish consistency is the hobgoblin of little minds." Every member should voice a reaction.

Next, critics should begin observing specifics causing the reactions and feelings that were voiced: "See where he describes the egg frying and how his eyes hurt?" or "Tell me why you liked the description; I didn't even particularly notice it." Questions of clarification should be raised: "Who is this Harlequin guy?" or "Why is the word *numbing* repeated so many times?" Literary terms and literary criteria should come into the discussion: "I think *numbing* has to do with use of alliteration, maybe it's even onomatopoeia, in the poem. Look at all the *n* and *m* sounds."

Finally, it is time to deal directly with the evaluation form. One person should take responsibility for filling out the copy of the evaluation form that will actually be stapled to the manuscript and accompany it through the filing system. This person will record the group's decisions. She might begin with, "OK, what score should we give this work for content?" Discussion, or maybe intense debate, will follow. The objective is for the group, like a jury, to arrive at a group agreement. The quality of the process will be compromised if all the group does is vote, no matter how the staff has set up your evaluation forms.

If, for example, three people on a committee want to award a 3 (out of 5) for the content, and two people want to award a 5, it makes no sense to award a 3 simply because more people voted for that score. Think about it: Three people are saying that the content of the work is quite average. A 3 is only 60 percent of the total possible. Two others are saying that the content of the work is outstanding. Giving the work a 4, by averaging the scores, does not reflect the critics' views either. Rather than simply voting, this committee needs to discuss the work further.

If debate becomes deadlocked or too heated, table the work for a while, and return to it at a different time. In a firm deadlock, it may eventually fall to those in the minority to decide that all views have been aired, that they have not been able to win their point, and that the view of the majority should prevail.

AVOIDING THE RUTS

Once your staff has carefully established basic procedures for debating the merits of manuscripts, you will be on the road to successful critiquing. That road will probably have a few ruts and potholes, though, such as the typical ones that follow. Try to avoid them.

Backtracking on the Decision

Once the evaluation form is filled out and the group's decision made, that decision should be final. "Can't we look at that story again?" is a question that can cost valuable time and undermine the sincere efforts that went into making the original decision. Unless the committee recommends that the manuscript be revised by the author, its evaluation is challenged by an editor or advisor, or special circumstances arise, the decision of the critics should be final.

If too many or too few manuscripts are being accepted overall, review the manuscripts that fall just above or below the breaking point for acceptance, however that breaking point is determined. Consider changing the breaking point; this is certainly fairer and more efficient than reevaluating manuscripts already critiqued.

Assuming the Author Is Not Sincere

Always assume that the author's effort is a sincere one, the best he can do. Treat that sincerity with the respect it deserves. You might find yourself thinking, "He didn't really try; I can tell he dashed this off in about ten minutes." If the work is poorly crafted, prove your conclusion with specifics from the work itself, but do not judge the author's sincerity. What appears to be quickly done sometimes hides subtle craft. Also, you would have difficulty proving a direct relationship between how long it takes to produce a creative work and the quality of that work. Handel wrote the entire *Messiah* in 23 days.

Forcing Discussion of an Unpromising Manuscript

It may be natural to feel that the staff owes a certain minimum amount of discussion to each manuscript. Critics may find themselves digging for things to say about a manuscript with little promise, just to satisfy the basics of fair critiquing. Do not do this. If the staff has read a work

You would have difficulty proving a direct relationship between how long it takes to produce a creative work and the quality of that work. Handel wrote the entire *Messiah* in 23 days.

individually and not a single person in the group finds it worth discussing, go on to the next manuscript quickly. That manuscript has had the benefit of several individual readings; it has gotten a fair trial.

Name-Calling and Labeling

Words like *junk*, *mindless*, and *ignorant* do not show respect for the author's honest attempt. Avoid negative one-word judgments and name-calling. When words like this are hanging in the air, the atmosphere for critiquing can become unhealthy.

Avoid negative one-word judgments and name calling.

Failing to Utilize Technical Terms

If literary terms are not heard in critiquing sessions, chances are that at least one of three problems has developed: 1) The level of discussion has not shifted naturally from reactions based on personal preferences to reactions stimulated by the work itself; 2) the discussion of the work is being conducted in very general terms rather than meaningful specifics; or 3) only the content of the work is being discussed—craft, style, and structure are being ignored.

Lincoln-Douglas Debating

Sometimes group discussion shifts to an intense debate involving only two group members. If such a debate helps to clarify and resolve two basic viewpoints being considered by the whole group, it is helpful. If such a debate is merely keeping the rest of the group from proceeding with discussion of the work at hand, it is not helpful. If you find yourself involved in such a debate, stop after a couple of minutes and ask the group, "Is this helping?" If you find yourself listening to such a debate, break in, tactfully but firmly, and ask the whole group, "Is this helping?"

Ignoring Quiet Group Members

Some people are quieter than others. In a critiquing group, though, some people may be silent for long periods of time, and their silence can act as a time bomb. Imagine nearing the end of a critique and suddenly having a previously silent group member say, "I still like this essay; we should print it." Suppose the evaluation form shows a low score. Avoid such awkward situations by periodically asking for the opinions of quieter group members.

Some people may be silent for long periods of time, and their silence can act as a time bomb.

THE CHALLENGE PROCESS

There will be times when an editor or advisor does not agree with the decision of the critiquing committee. Before such disagreement happens, develop a process for dealing with challenges. This way, particularly if tempers get hot, an agreed-upon process will help insure fair treatment of the editors, advisor, critics, and author.

Your challenge process might have several steps, including making an opportunity for the editor or advisor to discuss the work with the critics, seeking input from outside experts on literature, putting the issue to an all-staff vote, and identifying legal considerations that may override the staff's decision. You will want to refer to "Handling Sensitive Issues," pages 62–66, which includes discussion of legal considerations.

Questions and Activities

1. How would you add to or alter the basic critiquing procedure to fit your staff?
2. In Chapter 1, the section on staff votes outlines reasons for establishing quorum (page 13) and closing meetings to non-staff members (page 14). How might these reasons apply to groups critiquing manuscripts?
3. List the seven critiquing problems (ruts or potholes) listed in this section.
4. Other than the critiquing problems listed, is there a critiquing problem that you think your staff might encounter? What solution for this problem would you suggest?
5. Outline a challenge process for your staff. Be prepared to defend your process's practicality.

FINDING QUALITY IN A LITERARY WORK

In becoming a literary magazine staff member, you probably expected intense involvement with literature. In debating the merits of manuscripts, you have it. Did you also expect the frustration?

WHAT YOU *ARE* LOOKING FOR

> **Quality can be easy to visualize in your mind and frustrating to find on paper.**

Issues of quality are sometimes hard to resolve. Quality can be easy to visualize in your mind and frustrating to find on paper. Finding quality is an issue you cannot ignore, though, because you still have the job of deciding which manuscripts to print. Those manuscripts should be manuscripts of quality.

You are looking for works with solid content, controlled craft, a sense of style, evidence of creativity, and real impact on the reader. This search for quality can be particularly frustrating in student works, in which the author may achieve excellence in one area and not in another. Such is the nature of quality: Few successes are total.

By now your staff has assessed each staff member's preparation for finding quality, established objective criteria, and organized a good forum for debating literature. It is now your job as a literary critic to find and defend what you see as quality.

WHAT YOU ARE *NOT* LOOKING FOR

As a literary critic, it can help to know what you are looking for and also what you are not looking for. Dependence on certain characteristics can compromise quality. Here are a few.

Clichés

A cliché is an overused phrase or idea. It has popped up so often in speaking and writing that it has lost its impact. The reader reads right through a cliché, its familiarity robs a thought of impact, and the idea it expresses is pale and generic.

> **Writers generally should avoid clichés—like the plague.**

Sometimes a writer can use a cliché well. Dialogue, for example, with a few clichés like "jump the gun," "eyes like saucers," and "never too late," may sound pleasantly conversational because people talk that way. A writer might even overload a character's dialogue with clichés to show that the character is not an original thinker. Sometimes a cliché can be used humorously. However, writers generally should avoid clichés—like the plague.

Staff members have different skills and preparation levels for evaluating manuscripts. Take advantage of the diversity of resources within your staff.

Derivative Literature

> 'Twas the night before finals
> and all through the school
> the students were studying
> 'cause that was the rule.

Takeoffs such as this one, of "The Night Before Christmas," are about 5 percent original. Mimicry alone is not a significant accomplishment in literature, but mimicry can be done to different degrees. A story which is a takeoff of a familiar fairytale or currently popular TV show, for example, might introduce new and unique elements to a familiar formula.

Sometimes, without intending humor or commentary, an author mimics just the language or style of a known author, trying to sound like someone else rather than speaking with her own, unique voice. Such a derivative work would score poorly in a critique of style as well as of creativity.

If a takeoff is a successful mixture of mimicry and originality with a purpose, then the work may be parody, satire, or allegory. These are subgenres to balance with others in your magazine.

Plagiarism

Plagiarism is the act of claiming someone else's work as your own. A plagiarized work should not be considered for publication. Plagiarism includes stealing unique ideas as well as exact words. Plagiarism is illegal and immoral. Occasionally it is unintentional; usually it is not. Fortunately, a thorough group critiquing process allows many opportunities for plagiarism to be identified.

Writing as Personal Therapy

In times of intense emotion, people often turn to writing and work their feelings out on paper. William Wordsworth, a Romantic poet, valued highly the role of emotion in giving flight to the imagination. He spoke of good poetry as "the spontaneous overflow of powerful feelings." He also, though, spoke of the need of the poet, or presumably any writer, to begin composition "from emotion recollected in tranquility."

A writer must bring about a meaningful interplay of emotion, content, and craft. A work which begins as just an emotional outpouring may need several rewrites before that emotion becomes an inseparable part of the work's content and craft. Therapeutic works show themselves through their raw emotion: "He's wonderful, he's mine forever!" or "Why me?" or "Why did you leave me?" Anyone could relate to such emotions, but specific sense data and specific, well-developed characters are often missing. Only emotion speaks. The work needs control of content, which is often bland or obvious, and craft, which is often lacking. Works of this sort are likely possibilities for revision, if the author is willing.

Such works, even when well crafted, can be sentimental literature, which indulges in emotion for emotion's sake. The death of a sparrow and remembering your first kiss can be emotional experiences, but they need not be overly emotional. In sentimental literature, the author's objective is, inappropriately, to cause an emotional response, rather than to share honestly an emotional experience. The sentimental author tries to milk tears from the reader. Writers should have some control over their emotions, as a speaker giving a eulogy at a funeral must, but the sentimental author has none. Additionally, sentimental emotions are simplistic, reducing complex human emotions to clichés like: "and a single tear rolled down his cheek" or "with her by his side, he knew he was complete."

Predictable or Forced Rhyme

Have you ever heard a big tree falling after the logger's final stroke? The action is an inevitable, slow-motion sequence. The splintering and creaking racket stops only when the tree finally crashes onto the forest floor. A predictable rhyme has the same effect on the reader. Rather than sounding as a pleasing and natural outcome to a line, a predictable rhyme can be anticipated a dozen words ahead, creaking in the reader's head until it crashes inevitably in the ear.

> On slippery summer nights I hear a tune.

(Do you hear the word *moon* coming up? Or maybe *June*?)

> He knew that violence wasn't right
> and anger was for fools

(Do you hear the words *fight* and *rules* coming up?)

A rhyme that the reader can anticipate lines away is a rhyme that only does the obvious in sound and meaning. Predictable rhymes may be a signal, too, that the content of the poem itself is too obvious. In either case, such rhymes can weaken poetry.

A related problem is forced rhyme. A forced rhyme ignores grammar or natural word order to force a rhyming word into the needed po-

> **Therapeutic works show themselves through their raw emotion: "He's wonderful, he's mine forever!" or "Why me?" or "Why did you leave me?"**

> **A predictable rhyme can be anticipated a dozen words ahead, creaking in the reader's head until it crashes inevitably.**

sition. Song lyrics often turn phrases like "between you and me" into "between you and I," so that *I* can rhyme with *eyes*, *sky*, or whatever. The public seems willing to tolerate some of this, but forced rhymes can rob a poem of clear expression and freshness.

> "My suit!" he grinned. "Fresh pressed. Brand new."
> But frisbeed-flat his hat she threw.

Most of us would say "she threw his hat."

Stuffiness

An author should call on a large vocabulary to express himself, but when he calls on more vocabulary power than he needs, the effect is bad. Big words or high-sounding phrases for their own sake become attention-getters that distract from the real purpose of a work. An author who tries to impress with overly elegant language will only sound stuffy and artificial.

Poor Ratio of Length to Quality

It may not be fair, but the longer a work is, the more quality it needs to have to demand space in your magazine. If yours is a 40-page magazine, for example, a five-page play takes about 12 percent of your total space. Such a play had better rate more than the minimum standard for acceptance if it will take about one-eighth of the available space! Consider the ratio of length to quality in critiquing the longer works submitted.

Bathroom Humor

Bathroom humor refers to literature that relies, for its entertainment value, on any of the natural functions of the human body. Certainly you do not want to print anything in poor taste. The issue here might not even be one of poor taste, though, as much as one of inappropriate audience. Bathroom humor has the potential to offend part of your reading audience. Why risk offending even a few readers with a work having little serious purpose? Bathroom humor is not a literary genre to share with the wide reading audience you want your magazine to have.

Why risk offending even a few readers with a work having little serious purpose?

Questions and Activities

1. What are two frustrations you have had or expect to encounter in finding quality in literature? How will you deal with these frustrations?
2. List the eight characteristics that rob a work of quality. Can you think of any other such characteristics?
3. Here is a note from one friend to another. How many clichés does it contain? On your own paper, write out a listing of all the clichés you find.

> June 21, 9 A.M.
> Dear Lois,
>   This morning we have been merely ships that pass in the night, so I have stuck my neck out and taken the liberty of proceeding in full swing to keep the ball rolling on our 4th of July project. I have kept my nose to the grindstone, but it's really

no skin off my nose if you don't like what I've written. It may not be worth the paper it's written on, so we'll put our heads together, rack our brains, and come up with a great play for the 4th of July picnic.

I'm sorry I haven't accomplished more, but I've had too many irons in the fire lately. But, while many times I've felt like throwing in the towel, to tell the truth, I'm glad we decided to do this.

See you tomorrow morning,
Shantae

4. Examine the batch of sample manuscripts in Appendix A. Can you find in any of them examples of what you are *not* looking for?

BALANCING SUBJECTS, GENRES, AND AUTHORS

Chapter 3 to this point has discussed why quality should be the primary reason for printing one manuscript and not printing another. Unfortunately, however, choices by quality alone could result in some oddly balanced magazines.

Consider this circumstance: A community is ravaged by a tornado. It is theoretically possible that all the best literature by students that year could be about tornadoes. Should a literary magazine be all about tornadoes? In another circumstance, choices by quality alone could result, theoretically, in a magazine of all poetry and no other genre. Suppose, finally, that Leo Tolstoy attended your school, submitted works to your magazine, and your staff chose works on the basis of quality alone.

All about tornadoes, all poetry, or all by Tolstoy: These are extreme examples of imbalance in choice of subjects, genres, and authors. Balance contributes to excellence in a literary magazine. Quality of literature comes first, but do not ignore balance.

BALANCING SUBJECT MATERIAL

A range of subjects are perennial favorites in literary magazines: sunsets and sunrises; views of the mountains or the ocean; the love of a man and a woman; the death of a loved one; pets; friendship and loss of friendship. Under the pressure of critiquing, many works on subjects like these will fail to make the cut. The commonness of subject material will work against them, particularly in the scoring of creativity, unless the author has taken a unique approach. Take the best, eliminate the rest. If your submissions tend to show a narrow range of subject matter, bolster your publicity campaign, seeking more manuscripts from more students. If your magazine displays only works on predictable subjects, your readers will stereotype your publication. "Yep," they will say, "that's the kind of stuff you find in literary magazines."

Other than perennial favorites, some subjects may appear often as a reflection of a real, current concern among the student body: hotly de-

bated school issues, current social issues, a startling local event, or an emotional national event. Choose the best works you can find on a subject of current concern, but not to the exclusion of other subjects. Consider creating a special section in your magazine focusing on a current concern. Be sure to include a variety of viewpoints and reactions. Creative literature can be a powerful tool to help readers think through and resolve their feelings.

BALANCING GENRES

"What's in the literary magazine this year?"
"Oh, the usual. Poems and stories."

Including a wide variety of genres will please readers and keep them from becoming complacent. Much of what was just said about balancing subject material also applies to balancing genres. In Chapter 2 you were encouraged to solicit for a wide variety of genres and subgenres. As an activity in that section, you brainstormed a list of genres your staff would like to encourage. If, as submissions arrive, few genres on your listing are represented, use the strategies outlined for balancing subject material. Additionally, promising manuscripts of unusual genres might be worth revising or worth awarding extra points, as discussed on pages 48–50.

BALANCING NUMBER OF WORKS BY ONE AUTHOR

"None of my stories got in at all. How come this guy gets *seven* of his poems printed?"

This author feels hurt that none of her works was printed. She also has a legitimate gripe. Even if an author is excellent, you may want to limit how much is printed by one author. Seven works by one author

Final Pointers on Balance

- Do not stereotype the reading interests of your student body. They care about more than sports, dates, and rock and roll. Students will care about a wide range of subjects if they are presented with relevance to students.

- Every work in your magazine does not need to appeal to every reader. Shopping malls have specialty shops that are successful even though only a selected group goes there.

- Your magazine needs "anchors." In a mall, large department stores often act as anchors. Anchors are stores with general appeal, placed at critical locations to draw the public down all the major walkways of a mall. Your magazine needs a few works that will appeal to a wide reading audience and will be placed prominently to draw your readers through your magazine.

> **Given an outstanding author, your task is to represent her work well, not to overrepresent it.**

looks particularly self-indulgent if the author is a staff member for a magazine attempting to represent the entire student body. If your staff is choosing the best of each author who submits, you already have a strategy with limits. Staffs using other strategies for choosing manuscripts, however, may find it advantageous to set a limit.

The limit might be a number of manuscripts that you will print by one author. The limit might be the total number of column inches you will print by one author. Once your staff has decided how wide your columns will be, a column inch is one vertical inch of that column. The limit also might be the total number of manuscripts *and* artworks you will print by one person, because some authors are also artists.

Common objections to such limits include "But we should print *quality* first!" and "Everyone will *love* her stories!" Given an outstanding author, your task is to represent her work well, not to overrepresent it. Overrepresentation will hurt the quality of your magazine as a whole.

Excellent authors will feel well-represented by about three of their works. In fact, some might be embarrassed if you print more. All authors who submit works for consideration will appreciate your fairness. Readers will enjoy a wider representation of authors. Setting a limit will also push your staff to run the best possible campaign for soliciting manuscripts.

Questions and Activities

1. What do you feel is the appropriate relationship in a literary magazine between quality of literature and balance of subject matter, genres, and authors?
2. How will your magazine balance subject matter, genres, and authors?

YOUR MAGAZINE, AUTHORS, ARTISTS, AND COPYRIGHT

> **Your staff probably wants one-time rights, the right to print the work only in the current issue.**

When a student submits a work to a literary magazine staff, she understands that she is giving permission for her work to be printed. Like an author selling a work to a commercial magazine, she has just granted the staff nonexclusive rights. According to copyright law *nonexclusive rights* are the rights given when the author or artist sells a work to a collective work and there has been no other agreement made, in writing, with the publisher. A literary magazine, having many contributors, is a collective work.

Nonexclusive rights means that your magazine has permission to print the work in current and future issues. This permission is probably broader than your staff needs. What your staff probably wants is *one-time rights*, the right to print the work only in the current issue.

By law, the author or artist is the owner of what he creates. It is his property, like a house or a car. He does not own the ideas or information his work contains; those cannot be copyrighted. He does, however, own the unique expression that he has created. He may sell his work as he chooses. No one may print it, reproduce it, or perform it without his permission. He owns it for the length of his life plus 50 years. He has this protection, or copyright, whether or not he decides to register his work with the Copyright Office. On his work, he may write *Copyright 1991 by Jason McMillan* to show that he owns it. Believe it or not, copyright violations are rare.

Your magazine may have a copyright of its own, covering the editing and compilation of works in the magazine. Your magazine's copyright may complicate the rights of those who contribute.

First, if your magazine does not display a copyright notice, including the word *copyright* or the symbol ©, anyone who infringes on your contributors' copyright cannot be held accountable. Without a copyright notice, no one can know that the author or artist wished to maintain copyright.

Second, if your magazine does not display copyright, after five years all works become part of the public domain, a legal territory in which anyone can use the works without penalty. If the magazine does not display copyright, then authors and artists must register their copyright independently to protect their work.

Third, if your magazine *does* display copyright without any qualification, it maintains nonexclusive rights. This makes the works more difficult for your authors and artists to sell to other markets.

For these reasons, it is wise to print a statement modeled on the following in your magazine's introductory material:

> Copyright 1991 by DISTANT THUNDER, a publication of Southwest High School. After first publication, all rights revert to the author/artist. The views expressed herein do not necessarily reflect those of the DISTANT THUNDER staff or of Southwest High School.

This statement protects your magazine, authors, and artists, granting them full control of works after you have used them. The year given should be the year of publication. The concluding part of the statement simply reinforces the common assumption that authors and artists in a literary magazine express their individual views, not the views of the magazine in which they appear.

If you decide to register your magazine with the Copyright Office, send a form SE, the registration fee, and two copies of your magazine to Register of Copyrights, Library of Congress, Washington, DC 20559. (You may write for forms or call 202-479-0700.) Each issue must be registered separately.

If your magazine displays copyright but does not choose to register, the law still demands that you deposit two copies of each issue with the copyright office. Send two copies and a cover letter to the address just given. Explain that you are depositing these copies in compliance with section 407 of the copyright law. This must be done within three months of publication.

> **Without a copyright notice, no one can know that the author or artist wished to maintain copyright.**

Questions and Activities

1. What is the difference between nonexclusive and one-time rights?
2. Who may legally use the copyright symbol?
3. What are three complications for authors and artists that a magazine causes by not displaying a copyright notice?

- Are there campus-wide or school board policies about student publications or self-expression that must be reflected in your magazine's policy statement?
- What are the goals of your literary magazine?
- Who is eligible to submit works for consideration to your literary magazine?
- How will the staff handle creative works with possibly controversial content, such as: profanity; excessive violence; sex; plagiarism; violation of copyright; disrespect for the law; invasion of privacy; disrespect for the community's moral standards; advocation of illegal activities; and bigotry toward any race, sex, ethnic group, age group, or religion?
- What will be the relationship among staff members, editors, the advisor, any advisory board, and the administrators in handling controversial emotional, ethical, and legal issues?

Journalists in a free society have tremendous freedom of expression.

A police officer steps to the door of a brick bungalow. He stares at the familiar "5066" on the door as he nervously jams a finger at the doorbell. He is about to tell a woman that her husband, his partner, has been killed on duty. He scuffs at the rattan mat, waiting for her to answer, painfully rehearsing exactly what he will say. He knows that every word, every facial expression, every gesture that he is about to make will be written in this woman's memory for a lifetime.

Like the officer, your literary magazine staff may find itself in the position of handling a sensitive issue. This section discusses the emotional, ethical, and legal issues your staff may encounter.

WRITING AN EDITORIAL POLICY STATEMENT

When the police officer approached the door, he had guidelines from his department about notifying family members of a death. Such guidelines were probably reassuring at the time. Likewise, your magazine staff should have guidelines, called an *editorial policy statement*, on file and ready to guide you when sensitive issues arise. This policy statement should be written by the staff, reviewed by the staff yearly, and revised as needed. Ideally, it should also be reviewed and approved by the school administration.

Before you develop your policy statement, ask other publications and schools for samples of theirs. Samples may be available from your state's department of education. You might want to request a copy of the Code of Ethics of the Society of Professional Journalists, Sigma Delta Chi, 53 W. Jackson Blvd., Suite 731, Chicago, IL 60604. Samples may also be requested from the Student Press Law Center, 800 18th Street NW, Suite 300, Washington, DC 20006.

DEALING WITH ETHICAL DECISIONS

In dealing with all the questions given, your staff will wrestle with ethical decisions. Ethical decisions do not involve what you as a staff *can* do, because that is the area of law. Ethics involve what you *should* do, in the best interests of your magazine, readers, and society. Journalists in a free society have tremendous freedom of expression. Because this freedom gives tremendous power to their profession, journalists must reach for the highest ethical standards. Journalists must try to treat all segments of society with fairness and approach all subjects with a sense of fair play. For student journalists, this freedom is legally restricted in only five areas. These five areas are discussed in the following section, "Dealing with Legal Issues."

For the literary magazine journalist, ethical decisions can be complicated by the nature of literature and art itself. When an *author* treads on a sensitive area, perhaps offending the community's moral standards or advocating an illegal activity, ethics demand that the author's work be revised or rejected. What about *characters*, though, who tread on a sensitive area? Certainly people of this sort exist, and authors should have options for portraying them in literature. Huckleberry Finn, for example, in Mark Twain's masterwork, is a bigot. Early in the novel, both his language about and treatment of Jim clearly demonstrate Huck's bigotry. Also clear, however, is Twain's disapproval. Significantly, Huck, who is white, changes as a result of his adventures, and Jim, who is black, becomes a close friend.

Suppose your magazine had the opportunity to print a short story with a character and theme like *Huckleberry Finn*. Ethically, should you? To answer, your staff would have to determine standards of fairness and good taste by asking yourselves:

- Are the sensitive characters, images, actions, or ideas presented within a work that is otherwise acceptable to community values?
- Have most readers of our magazine been exposed to enough information about the sensitive issue that they can judge the significance of this creative work appropriately?
- Will most readers of our magazine accept the sensitive issue as a real part of life that is purposefully and tastefully explored in this piece of literature or art?

If the answer is "no" to any of these three questions, your staff probably should seek revisions or not print the work in question. Humor, including techniques like overstatement and caricature, is another quality of literature and art that can complicate ethical decisions. Ask of a humorous work the three questions just given, understanding that a work need not be serious to be purposeful.

Ambiguity in literature is yet another quality that can complicate ethical decisions. *Ambiguity* is the state of uncertainty resulting when there are several possible interpretations. Ambiguity can result from faulty expression: The author has simply failed to communicate clearly. Ambiguity can result from faulty reading: The reader has failed to correctly interpret what the author, perhaps subtly, has said. Ambiguity also can be the author's reflection of life; life, indeed, does contain ambiguities.

Presumably, the critiquing process would eliminate works that are ambiguous due to faulty expression. What happens, though, when an author deals with a sensitive issue ambiguously? A poem, for example, might discuss drugs as enhancers of creativity. If the poem leaves unclear the final, devastating effects of drug usage on creativity and on an individual's life, should you print it? Each work your staff encounters will be unique. Your staff would have to ask the three questions asked about *Huckleberry Finn*.

> Humor, including techniques like overstatement and caricature, is a quality of literature and art that can complicate ethical decisions.

DEALING WITH LEGAL ISSUES

For student journalists, freedom of expression is legally restricted in five areas, four of which also apply to professional journalists. Know these areas so that your staff can act responsibly in handling sensitive legal issues.

Libel

Libelous material is printed material that is both false and damages a person's reputation. Libel laws are complicated, subtly changing, and vary from state to state. Libel can occur in art or literature, whether fiction or nonfiction. Basically, a publication accused of libel must prove that the information printed is true, whereas the person claiming libel must prove that the information damaged her reputation, that it was read by third parties, that it refers to her specifically (even if she was not named specifically or a false name was used), and that your magazine acted negligently in printing the material.

The best defense against libel is truth, but truth must be proven by citing facts and sources. For a literary magazine, issues of truth and accuracy are complicated by the ambiguity in creative works and the wide range of techniques (irony, caricature) an author or artist might employ. Truth, most often, must be proven to a jury, and juries consist of average folks, not literary experts.

A second defense against libel is known as *fair comment and criticism*. When reviewing books, movies, concerts, recordings, restaurants, art exhibits, and other *public* entertainment, or when commenting on people in *public* life, criticism may be made as long as it is not malicious (ill-intentioned) and is factually accurate. Private individuals may not be criticized in the same way as public figures. (See "Invasion of Privacy" below.) Because libel is usually a civil offense, the penalty most often is money to be paid.

Invasion of Privacy

Revealing actual facts about people's personal lives without their consent is unethical. It can also be illegal and your magazine can be sued. Elected officials and public figures, because they are newsworthy, give up much of their legal right to privacy. Even private individuals, when involved in a newsworthy event, give up some privacy, because facts about their private lives that relate to the newsworthy event may be made public.

Use common sense in avoiding sensitive personal material. Double-check works revealing personal information. Is the information totally fictitious, or is there someone mentioned whose permission you should seek? Double-check with any author who has revealed much private information about himself. Be sure he actually submitted the work for consideration and intends that it be made public. Always be sensitive to the privacy of students, families, and faculty who have experienced trauma or tragedy, even if it might be newsworthy and an appropriate subject for literature or art.

In illustrating literature, particularly with photos, be careful not to cast any subject in a false light. You cannot without permission, for example, illustrate an essay on anorexia nervosa with a photo of one of your school's very thin gymnasts. If she is anorexic, you have invaded her privacy. If she is not anorexic, you have cast her in a false light, which is illegal.

Obscenity

U.S. courts have wrestled for years to find a definition of *obscenity*. The First Amendment does not cover language that is vulgar, profane, or obscene. But what language is that, and in what context? Interestingly, a literary work is the context in which offensive language might be most acceptable to some readers. The swearing of John Steinbeck's farmhands, for example, adds historical detail to his portrayals of the farm workers and their lives. Such language certainly does not belong in a letter to the editor, nor in the hands of readers too young to understand its purpose. Some feel such language does not belong in the hands of any reader.

When your staff evaluates possibly obscene material, avoid defining *obscenity* and simply ask, "Will our readers be offended by this?" and "Does the language in question have a definite purpose?" If in doubt, leave the material out.

> **Use common sense in avoiding sensitive personal material. Double-check works revealing personal information.**

Substantial Disruption
Journalists may not publish material intending to cause illegal activities or violence. Additionally, student journalists may not publish or distribute materials in such a way as to cause substantial disruption of the educational process. Your staff, then, may not publish a work seriously advocating that students stop doing all homework nor burst into classrooms unannounced to distribute magazines.

Administrative Editorial Control
The Supreme Court's 1988 decision in *Hazelwood School District v. Cathy Kuhlmeier, et al.* established new powers for school administrators in controlling student expression. The complete decision runs about 40 typed pages. Its basic ruling is that school administrators may restrain (prohibit publication, edit, censor, exercise prior restraint over) any writing that they feel is not consistent with the "basic educational mission" of a school.

Prior to the *Hazelwood v. Kuhlmeier* decision, school administrators could exercise restraint only over writing that violated one of the other four legal areas just discussed. The Court's decision applies to all student publications. To exercise the powers granted in *Hazelwood v. Kuhlmeier*, administrators may choose to use their right of prior review, that is, reading and approving the content of the literary magazine before it is printed.

The broad phrase "basic educational mission" allows administrators control over both content and style. They may restrict writing that is "ungrammatical, poorly written, inadequately researched, biased or prejudiced, vulgar or profane, or unsuitable for immature audiences." In the Hazelwood School District, the principal removed from the school's newspaper stories about students who became pregnant and a report on the impact of parents' divorces on students. The principal, Robert Reynolds, felt the stories were unfair, invaded privacy, and were inappropriate for younger teenagers.

The police officer mentioned earlier had to decide if he was the right person to tell his partner's wife. Likewise, your staff may debate whether your magazine is the right forum for sensitive material. The officer knew the quality of his telling would mark a line between compassion and insensitivity. So, too, your staff's handling of sensitive material may mark a line between ethical and unethical, legal and illegal.

> **Your staff may debate whether your magazine is the right forum for sensitive material.**

ESTABLISHING AN ADVISORY BOARD

An advisory board is a group of people with expertise who care about student expression. You might want to establish an advisory board for your magazine or for all your school's publications. You might even consider one for all school organizations concerned with the ethics, quality, and legality of student expression in written or spoken form.

Members of your advisory board might include your editors and advisor, editors and advisors of other publications, representatives from your student government and other school groups, school administrators, parents, concerned citizens, civic leaders, legislators, artists and graphic designers, and local journalists and lawyers.

Establishing a board says that your magazine thinks carefully about ethics and the law. This act and a good track record for responsible journalism are your magazine's best defenses against unfair censorship or control. Community members and school administrators who have worked with you on an advisory board and seen your responsible record will be more likely to support your handling of sensitive issues. They will be more likely, too, to support a wider latitude of unusual forms and subjects for creative expression.

Questions and Activities

1. If your staff already has a policy statement, when was the last time the staff reviewed or revised it?
2. List three items that you feel should be included in your magazine's policy statement.
3. Discuss the legal and ethical concerns a staff might encounter in each of these situations:
   a. A magazine staff wants to print a story that the entire staff agrees is outstanding. A major character, however, liberally uses a particular word that the staff feels readers will find objectionable. In a conference, the author stated clearly that the objectionable word makes the character "authentic" and that the story would not "ring true" without it. He tells the staff it may not print the story without that word. What should the staff do?
   b. A student submits three excerpts from her diary powerfully describing three days of waiting for her father to return from dangerous military duty. The manuscript is riddled with nonstandard grammar and spelling errors. Part of the staff wants to edit the grammar and spelling as they would any other work. Others feel that such editing would rob the work of its unique sound and the real feeling of a personal diary. What should the staff do?
   c. Reliving the suicide attempt of a close friend, a student writes a poem about the attempt and includes images of his friend's childhood and recent home life. Although submitted anonymously, two staff members immediately identify the probable author and friend. What should the staff do?
   d. Staff members want to distribute to classes questionnaires about the possible content, format, and price of the upcoming issue of the literary magazine. The principal objects to class time being spent on these questionnaires, saying they are not academic in nature. What should the staff do?
   e. A staff wants to print a review of the latest book by a local author who will be speaking on campus two days after the magazine goes on sale. The review concludes that the author "would serve society better as an accountant, rather than as an author, given her obsession with meaningless details." Should the staff print the review?

TITLING MANUSCRIPTS

Good titles can help readers find what they want to read and stimulate them to read more. A good title is consistent with the tone, mood, and purpose of the manuscript and does not set expectations not met. For example, "Over Hill, Over Dale" might catch the reader's attention, but it would be too "cute" a title for a serious story about military combat.

- A striking statement: "It's Alive," "They're Freezing," "Peter Pan Has Flown Away"
- A provocative or paradoxical phrase: *Mr. Mom* or "Four Women in One Body" (the latter might be an essay about the four roles that the modern woman must play)
- A question: "Where Have the Children Gone?" "Is There Life After 40?"
- A paraphrase: "Home, Home Off the Range," *If Life's a Bowl of Cherries, What Am I Doing in the Pits?* "Pride Time"

- A word, phrase, or quotation from the manuscript itself: "Man on a List," "Energy Spent," "Catatonia," "We're Not in Kansas Anymore"
- A word or phrase suggested by the subject or theme: "Eulogy for John Belushi" (Belushi's name might not be mentioned directly), "Covenants" (poem about promises and bonds between people)
- A phrase including the genre of the work: "Ode on a Grecian Urn," "Preceding Dialogue"
- A rhyme, alliteration, or onomatopoeia: "The Broken Token,"

"Sixth Sense," "Winter Weather Warnings"
- A balance and contrast: *Rich Man, Poor Man; Run Silent, Run Deep*; "Fantasy Feature: Reality"; "The Hard Price of Soft Living"

When approaching an author to discuss the title of his work, explain the needs of a periodical for attention-getting titles. Bring a list of possible titles brainstormed by the staff and ask the author to either choose one or present his own alternative. Respect the author's right to stick with his own title (maybe he's right), and be prepared to live with a few titles like "Love" or "My Girlfriend."

Good titles are hard to find. Even professional authors fight to find the right title, and, often, it is the publishing staff who brainstorms the final, just-right title. Margaret Mitchell called her book *Tomorrow Is Another Day* before hitting on *Gone with the Wind*. Frank L. Baum's *The Wizard of Oz* was first known as *The Emerald City*.

Questions and Activities

1. See the sample manuscripts in Appendix A. What are the best titles you can brainstorm for manuscripts number 1, 3, 6, and 9? Work with a partner or in groups. Generate two or three possibilities for each manuscript.

TECHNIQUES FOR PROOFING

Proofreading or *proofing* refers to the process of checking a manuscript for mechanical exactness. Careful proofing is important to any journalistic product and particularly important to a literary magazine for two reasons.

First, poor proofing damages the staff's credibility. "If they can't even get the spelling right," a student may think, "how carefully did they choose what to print?" Authors, who must trust the staff to handle their works carefully, may be less likely to submit works to a magazine with a poor reputation for accuracy. The reading audience, too, may not take seriously a magazine with serious proofing problems. A staff

> **"If they can't even get the spelling right, how carefully did they choose what to print?"**

A staff that proofs carefully will not get credit for caring. Excellent proofing is simply the expected norm.

that proofs carefully, by the way, will not get credit for caring. Excellent proofing is simply the expected norm.

Second, the copy being proofed is creative work in which particular word choices may communicate through sound, rhythm, and imagery as well as through meaning. A misprinted word, then, can be destructive at several levels.

In producing a literary magazine, your staff will proof works at two different stages. First, you will proof the original manuscript before typesetting it. Then, you will proof the typeset copy before sending it to the printer.

PROOFING ORIGINAL MANUSCRIPTS

When your staff begins proofing manuscripts, have two or three staff members proof each manuscript. Do not rely on the eyes of a single person to weed out all errors.

Always have a dictionary and your staff's stylebook handy. Your dictionary should be a good, current collegiate or unabridged edition. A stylebook is whatever handbook your staff chooses to use to answer questions about mechanics. Your stylebook might be a grammar and composition textbook used in your school. Many journalists use *The Associated Press Stylebook*, *The Chicago Manual of Style*, or *The New York Times Manual of Style and Usage*.

Try reading each manuscript several times. Many specific readings may actually be accomplished faster than trying to read for everything in one reading.

In reading for spelling and capitalization, read from right to left, that is, backwards, to divorce mechanics from content. Spelling and capitalization errors may pop out quickly when you scan the line backwards, without being distracted by content.

Use a ruler when you proof, pulling it down the page as you read, to help you focus on the specifics and avoid hopping over a group of words.

Proofing Creative Writing

Creative writing bends the rules. Unusual spellings, sentence fragments, unorthodox punctuation, and nonstandard capitalization may all play a part in an author's attempt to communicate. On the other hand, a mechanical error may be just that. You may also confront attempts to bend the rules that do not work very well. Read with all these possibilities in mind. Most of the time, the author's intent will be clear, but if it is not, contact the author.

Be more cautious in making changes to poetry than any other genre. Capitalization and punctuation play major parts in texturing and directing a poem. Generally, leave punctuation and capitalization as the author has placed it. Consider changes only when an item causes real confusion or the item is oddly inconsistent within the poem. Although most mechanical corrections are routinely made by journalists without contacting the author, always consult the author before changing punctuation or capitalization in a poem.

Be more cautious in making changes to poetry than any other genre.

Marking Errors

Mark corrections in red so that the staff's corrections are distinct from any changes to the manuscript made by the author herself. In marking corrections, never obliterate what the author originally wrote. If some-

- Read once for spelling and capitalization.
- Read once for punctuation.
- Read once for homonyms. Look for words like these and be sure the author has used the one intended:

  your, you're

  its, it's

  to, too, two

  there, they're, their

  new, knew

  here, hear

- Read once for grammar. Check particularly for consistency in verb tenses, accuracy in pronoun usage, and complete sentences.
- Read once for content. Read for meaning, clarity, and logic. Watch out for unintentional malapropisms, like *precede* for *proceed* or *formally* for *formerly*.

one disagrees with your correction, the author's original choice must be readable. If an author's work is being handled as a computer file, be sure to store or print out a copy of the original before making on-screen changes.

Be sure to correct the error, not just mark it. Putting *sp.* next to a word does not tell anyone how it should be spelled. Use standard proofreading symbols, shown in Figure 3.8, to make corrections.

PROOFING TYPESET COPY

Typeset copy in this textbook refers to your final, printer-ready copy, whether done on a typewriter, computer printer, mimeograph master, or professional typesetting machine. It is this copy that you will send to the printer in final layouts. With typeset copy in hand, your job is to see that it matches the original from which it was set.

Good typesetters will deliver exactly what was requested. It is not their job to think for you. Their job is to respond exactly to your exact instructions. If you wrote *mlik*, you deserve to get *mlik* back, not the *milk* you thought you were requesting. Conversely, typesetters are only human, and no one is perfect at the keyboard. No matter how nice that typeset copy looks at first skimming, it contains errors. Here are strategies for finding them.

Have two or three staff members proof each typeset copy. Consider having one staff member read the copy out loud to another staff member who has the original in hand. Read everything, including punctuation marks, indents, and capitalization.

Scan the copy once from right to left, that is, backwards, to divorce mechanics from content. Some errors may pop out when you scan the line backwards, without being distracted by the content. In poetry, particularly, count the number of lines in the original and in the typeset copy to be sure they match—a common typesetting error is to skip a line. Then check for end repetitions. An end repetition is the common error of typing a word once at the end of a line and then accidentally repeating it at the beginning of the next line.

As you read, use a ruler or other guide. If you are proofing by yourself, use two—one for the original and one for the typeset copy. (For the

> **Good typesetters will deliver exactly what was requested. It is not their job to think for you. If you wrote *mlik*, you deserve to get *mlik* back, not the *milk* you thought you were requesting.**

typeset copy, use the edge of a clean sheet of paper, since a ruler might damage your copy.) Move the guides down the page as you check, matching line for line.

Mark errors on typeset copy only with a non-photo pen or pencil. "Non-photo" means that the marks will not be seen by the printer's camera. Methods for correcting typeset are outlined in Chapter 5, page 125. For desktop publishing systems, making corrections to the file and printing a new copy may be easiest, so it would not matter what you mark the typeset copy with. When you mark errors, use standard proofreading symbols (see Figure 3.8).

Figure 3.8
Copyediting Symbols

My hair was like a a field of ravens	delete
Seen on the moon are those who	delete and close up
They will see eldest cousins (my)	insert a word
Brnches of our family tree	insert a letter
out there for him. all you have	capitalize
and We headed to the car	lowercase
a thirty percent lower risk	set in numerals
across State Blvd.	spell out
from Big Deal, Incorporated	abbreviate
houses will be not in the future	transpose words
lazily sways across the playground	transpose letters
where raging fires crisp woodlands	separate words
what we were joking about stet	ignore copy mark; leave it alone
by Joanna McQueen	set in boldface
the Trumpet policy statement	set in italics
I'd never heard of a bald giraffe	paragraph
tomorrow.) "I know you thought too young to understand. He could	new paragraph
in Chen's office rang.	
He looked over at it, and	no paragraph; run in
I think, dream, search, smile	set flush left
by Lisa Rinker	set flush right
Photo Gallery	center copy
Also once the magazine	insert comma
and conserving resources. By	insert period
throwing erasers? he asked.	inset quotation marks
We dont want to defeat	insert apostrophe
the neverending, slick and snakey road	insert hyphen

Questions and Activities

1. Why is careful proofing particularly important to a literary magazine?
2. List five guidelines for basic proofing of an original manuscript.
3. What, particularly, should you watch for in proofing creative writing?
4. In the following poem by Emily Dickinson, how many errors are there in each line? On your own paper, write the word or words that need correcting and mark them with the appropriate proofreading symbols.

> My life closed twice before it's close;
>   It yet remains to see
> If Immorality unveil a
>   a third event to me,
>
> So huge, so hopeless to concieve,
>   As these that twice befell.
> Parting is all we now of heaven,
>   And all we need of hell.

CHAPTER FOUR

DESIGNING THE MAGAZINE

OVERLAPPING STAGES

Most literary magazine staffs cannot deal with publicity first, then critiquing, and then magazine design. Deadline pressure simply will not allow the luxury of handling one stage of production completely and then moving to the next. Chances are that, in a single-task approach, designing the magazine is a step that will be shortchanged. It is easy to think that a magazine can be designed while it is being put together to be printed. "We'll decide on how to do titles when we get to them," some might say. Careful design with real impact, however, needs to be planned before production begins.

As soon as manuscripts are being handled, your staff will probably find it advantageous to reserve a part of each week's meeting time for design discussions. This chapter will provide you with guidelines for magazine design and many design ideas.

Whether yours is a literary magazine or a literary-art magazine, careful design decisions will ensure that your final product has a "look" that is distinctive and appealing to readers. Your design decisions will range from the larger components, such as the cover, title page, and sequence of your magazine, to the smaller details, such as handling artists' credits and page numbers.

THE DESIGN CONCEPT

Suppose you walk into a doctor's waiting room where someone has left magazines scattered on a table. Two or three are lying open. Without reading anything in particular on the pages, you easily identify each of the open magazines. Why? Assuming these are magazines you have seen before, it is because each one *looks* like itself. Part of a magazine's look comes from the subject matter it contains, such as sports, food, current events, or poetry. Subject matter aside, though, a well-designed magazine has a distinctive look arising from the purposeful use of columns, placement of artworks, handling of titles, choice of typefaces (styles of type), and many other details. A distinctive look is the result of a carefully chosen and applied design concept.

GETTING THE CONCEPT

A design concept is something that guides a staff through all the visual decisions that must be made to produce a magazine. A design concept pulls together the staff's thinking and focuses that thinking on a distinctive result: your magazine's visual appearance. Do not confuse a design concept with a theme: Themes deal with content; design concepts deal with visual appearance. A theme purposefully sets limits on the content; a design concept aims to provide visual unity.

If you want your magazine to look the same issue after issue, your design concept will remain the same. If you want each issue to look different, you will modify your design concept for each issue. A design concept can take a number of forms:

> **Themes deal with content; design concepts deal with visual appearance.**

- A quotation from a student, from someone notable, or from great literature. A quote used as a design concept might appear on the front cover, back cover, or as a frontispiece. (See the discussion of frontispieces under "Introductory Components" on page 84.) The quote evokes a mental picture, the mood and subject of which are reflected in the magazine through many visual details. Examples: "We have nothing to fear but fear itself."—F.D.R.; "We're not in Kansas anymore."—Dorothy in *The Wizard of Oz*; "As dawn heralds today, so also is vision the harbinger of enlightened thought."—Roger Franson, student; "Words, words, words."—Hamlet in *Hamlet*; "Art retains all the peace the world has lost."—Michael Bailey, student; "A kinder, gentler nation."—George Bush.
- A subtitle for your magazine, appearing on the title page. As an element of the title page, the subtitle focuses on a particular idea that is the spirit of your magazine. Examples: RUBICON: The Artist's Dance; SCRIBE: Life Without the Ground; LION'S ROAR: Piece of Mind; IN A NUTSHELL: Oasis Logos.
- A logo. A logo is a shape or design that becomes the trademark of your magazine. A logo might be used in combination with a subtitle or stand by itself as a design concept. The shape might be drawn from nature, taken from some academic study, or created from scratch. The possibilities are infinite: circles, triangles, abstract inkblots, yin and yang, waves, flowers, animals, gears, and balloons, to name just a few. Figure 4.1 illustrates the use of a logo. A logo might appear on the cover, title page, table of contents, or other prominent places in the magazine. A logo is reproduced as the same image every time it is used, varying only in size or color. A logo might become part of

Figure 4.1
Logo

The staff of FROM THE DEPTHS (Lincoln Southeast H.S., Lincoln, NE) used a triangle as a logo. A Large, light blue version partially outlined in darker blue cuts through seven spreads in the magazine. A smaller, gray logo appears in the folio line and title page.

a folio line, the line on each page giving the page number, name of the magazine, and date.

- A grouping of key words. The group of words or phrases together creates a mood or attitude that is the soul of your magazine. Unlike other design concepts listed here, key words might not appear at all in a magazine. The words might act only as a guide for the staff in making visual decisions, and the spirit of those words would be in the look created by the staff's decisions. If the key words themselves do appear, they might be mentioned in an editor's note, in which an editor describes how the magazine came to be. Many commercial magazines are based on this approach. Examples: balanced, thin, clean, classic, calm; optimistic, mechanical, futuristic, technological, logical, detailed; graffiti, change, energy, now, the power of words, the people.

- A work of art or literature. Your staff might choose a work submitted to your magazine as the magazine's design concept. The work would be featured prominently, perhaps as a frontispiece (see page 84), and its tone, mood, and details would guide your magazine. The work's title could become the subtitle of your magazine.

- A dedication to someone or something your staff admires. (See page 85.) Examples: a piece of music; a painting; a special or fantastical place; a person whose creativity or commitment you admire; someone in today's paper.

- Something else. Your staff may think of a unique way to give your magazine a distinctive look. Be sure that whatever design concept you choose gives your staff a reasonable basis for making visual decisions.

USING THE CONCEPT

A design concept may take a form that makes it obviously visible in a magazine, as a frontispiece, subtitle, dedication, or other element. A design concept can do much more, though, than appear once or twice in your magazine. A good design concept helps your staff make many decisions. Here are examples of design concepts at work. Each example covers only a handful of the visual decisions a staff must make.

A staff chooses the key words *balanced, thin, clean, classic,* and *calm.* Staff members place the author's name to the left and the artist's name to the right below oversized titles. This creates a *balance* reminiscent of the triangular pediment topping a row of columns of a *classic* Greek temple. For prose, they emphasize the architectural feel of the page by giving the three narrow (*thin*) columns a *clean* edge with a *thin* line. At the bottom of the page, the name of the magazine and page numbers are in a *classic* typeface that reminds staff members of the Roman numerals on the cornerstones of buildings. The typeface they choose for titles is a modern one with *thin, clean* lines, *balanced* with a simple dot. Artworks are also bordered with a *clean, thin* line and no artworks bleed (extend off the page in one or more directions)—this suggests *calm* and *balanced.* The cover has only the title of the magazine against a background textured like *classic* white marble. (See Figure 4.2.)

Another staff decides to dedicate its magazine to the creative spirit of Vincent van Gogh. One staff member paints an artwork for the cover

A good design concept helps your staff make many decisions.

Figure 4.2
Mock-up for Design Concept with Key Words *Balanced, Thin, Clean, Classic, Calm*

**Figure 4.3
Mock-up for Design Concept
Based on van Gogh**

**Figure 4.4
Folio Line for van Gogh
Design Concept**

that combines images of whorling stars, sunflowers, and van Gogh's china-blue eyes, all subjects of van Gogh's paintings. Another staff member writes a paragraph dedicating the current issue to van Gogh. She focuses on his painting *Starry Night* and quotes from Anne Sexton's poem "The Starry Night" and Don McLean's song "Vincent," both inspired by van Gogh's painting. She points out that, like van Gogh, every author and artist struggles to communicate a unique vision of the world; ultimately, the influence of an artist's work on others can remain largely unknown to the artist. So it was for van Gogh and is for contributors to a literary magazine. Page numbers are set inside whorled stars, and the name of the magazine on the cover, title page, and folio line is handwritten in a style imitating how van Gogh signed his paintings. Layouts have only a little white space, because the staff decides that less white space is more in keeping with the style of van Gogh's paintings. Most artworks bleed in one direction to underscore the unbalanced aspects of van Gogh's life. (See Figures 4.3 and 4.4.)

Often, a design concept helps a staff choose among equally workable possibilities. "Where should we put our page numbers?" someone might ask. Page numbers can be in an outside corner, inside corner, or centered. They can be at the top, bottom, or side of the page. To decide which position works best, examine which one fits your design concept. A swirled, airy logo might imply a lightness that best places it and page numbers at the tops of pages. *Balanced* as a key word might imply a centered page number. "Words, words, words" might imply "numbers, numbers, numbers" and lead to a folio line that repeats the page number across the page (12 12 12 12 12).

Questions a Design Concept Can Answer

1. What will the shape and size of the magazine be?

2. What type of binding (staples, glue, other) will the magazine have?

3. On what color paper will the magazine be printed? Will the cover be printed on a different color paper? Will there be a second ink color (other than black) on the cover, or other uses of color in the magazine?

4. How will the folio line look? How large, in what style, and where on the page will folios (page numbers) be?

5. What typeface and size will be used for body copy?

6. What typeface, size, and placement will be used for authors' names? For artists' names?

7. Where will titles of literary works be placed? What typeface and size will they be? If there are variations in the appearance of titles, what guidelines will determine what is acceptable? Will artworks have titles? If so, what guidelines will determine their placement and look?

8. Is there a repeated design element, such as a line, box, or border, that can be used to enhance the design concept? What guidelines will determine acceptable use of this element?

9. What will the standard column width be? Will there be variations on the column width? If so, what guidelines will determine when to vary column width?

10. What other visual elements might give the magazine a sense of unity and flow from first page to last?

11. Who will design the cover and title page of the magazine and what guidelines will she have?

12. Where and in what format will the magazine give credit to the staff?

13. What will the table of contents look like, how much space will it take, and how can it enhance the design concept?

14. Will there be any optional components added to the opening of the magazine? A dedication? A frontispiece? Teasers or ears? What guidelines will determine the look of any added component?

15. How much space is needed for advertisers and patrons? Where will this space be in the magazine, and what guidelines will determine the look of this space?

16. Will there be any optional components added to the back of the magazine? An index? A eulogy? Special thanks? What guidelines will determine the look of any added components?

17. Will the magazine incorporate an endstop for longer works? If so, what will it look like and where will it be placed?

18. Will there be any special sections within the magazine, for example, focusing on a topic of special interest to students, on special artwork, or on a contest?

19. What guidelines will determine the sequence of literature and art from first page to last?

Use the design concept to guide decisions into a unified package. Some decisions may not lend themselves to interpretation through your design concept, but at least you can avoid conflicting with the decisions that really are guided meaningfully by the design concept.

Two things a design concept should not do are limit or dominate the content of a magazine. A staff should not find itself saying, "This short story is outstanding, but it doesn't go with the design concept. Maybe we shouldn't print it." This staff is confusing a design concept with a theme. A staff actually choosing a theme, such as "War reveals humanity's true nature" or "Adulthood is a do-it-yourself kit," will want all writers and artists to produce works based on that theme. All magazines need a design concept to guide visual appearance; many magazines need a theme to limit content. While commercial magazines usually have themes limiting their content and tone, it is less common for literary magazines to have specific themes.

A staff also should not use a design concept so that it dominates the content of a magazine. "Life's a circus" is a workable design concept, but it could get out of control. Imagine pages with festive balloons and grinning clowns' faces. Now imagine such a page with a deeply serious essay about nuclear waste. It doesn't work, does it? The design concept inappropriately dominates the content. Balloons and grins might work on a cover, but other images of the circus would better complement art and literature on pages within the magazine.

> A staff should not find itself saying, "This short story is outstanding, but it doesn't go with the design concept. Maybe we shouldn't print it."

Figure 4.5
Magazine Organized by
Sections

The CONTRABAND staff (Center H.S., Kansas City, MO) divided their magazine into four sections. Only the section headings appear in the table of contents.

FROM THE EDITOR'S TERMINAL...

Pssst! You now hold a copy of our third bundle of smuggled goods, Center's Literary Magazine, *Contraband*. Use it well. A lot has gone on in smuggling this package to you. For one, every aspect of this magazine has been done entirely by students, from the writing, to the typesetting, even down to the folding of the pages. We take pride in the fact that ours is a student-produced publication, with only advisory help from adults. Two adults in particular, Larry Bradshaw and Mary Lu Foreman have been instrumental in providing an underground haven for this operation and many long hours spent planning and executing our initiatives. Thanks, guys.

In this package, you'll find a wide variety of goods, ranging from Marchel Abner's look at black heritage, *Family Tree*, to *For Your Thighs Only*, Matt Loomis' parody of James Bond films. Additionally, we have composition teacher Chris Adams Prost's first attempt at fiction writing, *A Rustle of Leaves*.

In addition, we've strived to make our little bundle more aesthetically pleasing. Even though you supposedly can't judge a book by its cover, we'd like you to anyway. The two color cover design, created by Art Editor Andy Kallem is a break from our first two volumes, and is indicative of the unique designs you'll find on the pages within. Additional artwork was provided by Brian Burgdorf, Sonya Cox and Malcolm Edwards. If we've achieved our intended objective, you'll look at these unique designs and undergo a personal emotional

celebration. Or maybe it will all be subliminal. Anyway, we tried.

And we've tried before - and had success. The second issue of *Contraband* received the highest rating from the National Council of Teachers of English, as well as a first class rating from the Columbia Scholastic Press Association. We got into the international smuggling trade as well, leaving 100 or so copies of the '87 edition at the Little Heath Comprehensive School in Berkshire, England. In turn, they smuggled us a few copies of their magazine, *Sixth Sense*. A sister publication relationship was born.

As suggested by several people, we broke the book down into four sections by theme, Mixed Emotions, Trials and Triumphs, Sixth Sense, and A Matter of Life and Death. But nothing in life is easily classifyable, particularly the thoughts of individuals expressed in literature. For this reason, the overall theme, ''Beyond Definition'' was chosen to balance the individuality of the works with the classifications of the section divisions. Besides, ''Beyond Definition'' describes how of the operation of the magazine has gone, since its very inception. Appropriate.

Before we go, we'd like to take this opportunity to wish our long-time purveyor of smuggled goods, Chet Landes, well on his retirement from teaching. We've enjoyed his support during the past three years. Thanks Chet, and God....Bless America.

Well, here's your *Contraband*. Don't get caught.

Jeff Field
Editor in Chief

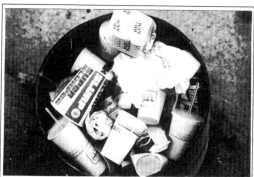

-Photo by Lori Tack

Mixed Emotions

-SMUGGLED WITHIN-

- 3 -

SEQUENCING LITERATURE

There are many ways to answer questions like ''What do we put first?'' and ''What comes next?'' Magazines are flip books: People tend to flip through them to find what interests them. In that sense, the sequence of literature and art in your magazine may not be as important as you think. How, though, does a staff sequence a magazine to keep the reader flipping and reading? Most organizational plans are a variation on one of three basic types: continuums, sections, or push-aparts. Some plans are blends of these types. Your design concept may or may not help make decisions about sequencing of content.

Continuums

A continuum is a continuous series, moving from beginning to end in a gradual flow. Some design concepts may imply a continuum. A clock-face used as a logo, for example, might imply a sequence from optimistic, forward-looking, sunny works (morning); to works of conflict, tension, and action (the heat of the day); and finally to reflective, calm, philosophical works (evening). In this continuum, works would be sequenced by their mood or tone, moving in a gradual flow from one tone into the next. No headings would divide one tone from another. Readers would probably become aware of such an organizational device only if an editor chose to mention it in an introductory note, or if a vis-

only if an editor chose to mention it in an introductory note, or if a visual element of the magazine, such as the folio line, gradually changed from beginning to end.

Other continuums might move from past to present to future; from humans in tune with nature to humans out of tune with nature; or from the individual to groups to society. Because a continuum establishes a general and subtle flow, works that at first don't seem to fit can usually be tucked in without disturbing the flow.

A continuum establishes a general and subtle flow.

Sections

Establishing sections in a magazine means finding a number of headings under which a staff can group all of its literature and art. The staff would make the sections evident in the table of contents and with section headings within the magazine (see Figure 4.5). A traditional approach is to group literature by genres: poetry, fiction, and nonfiction. Such a decision may have no direct association with a design concept. College literary magazines sometimes group by author or artist: poetry by Solveig Thompson, drawings by Lorenzo Little Spotted Horse.

Many plans for sections, though, spring directly from a design concept. If a magazine's subtitle is "Loving Mother Earth," there might be sections entitled "Earth," "Air," "Fire," and "Water." The PEGASUS Staff of Martin County High School, in Stuart, Florida, used the subtitle "Writings from the Edge" for one issue and created sections called "Learning Before the Edge," "Living on the Edge," and "Dreaming Beyond the Edge." The editor's introduction discussed the quality of being constantly "on the edge" of something in life.

A quote used on a frontispiece might be subdivided into sections. In Greek mythology, the Sphinx asks Oedipus, "What goes on four feet in the morning, two at noon, and three at night?" "Man," answers Oedipus. "Four in the Morning," "Two at Noon," and "Three at Night" could become section headings relating to the three stages of a human's, or perhaps an entire society's, life.

When using sections, be sure they allow placement of all your literature and art. Avoid catch-all sections like "Other Genres" or "Miscellaneous." These imply that your sections do not completely subdivide the content, and authors or artists who find themselves in a catch-all section may feel shortchanged. Readers may find such sections unexciting, too. A staff, for example, that has sectioned its magazine into "Poetry" and "Prose" may have trouble finding a reasonable placement for a musical composition. Be sure, also, that readers clearly understand the names of sections. Add an editor's comment or other explanatory information, if needed.

Push-Aparts

"The way we've got this set up, it looks like we'll be printing our two longest short stories right next to each other. Is that a good idea?" The staff member asking this question might advocate using push-aparts. Push-aparts allow a staff to distribute interest throughout the magazine and to avoid density of one element at one place in the magazine. A staff might use a push-apart strategy as its primary means of sequencing a magazine or use push-aparts within a continuum or within sections of a magazine.

Some elements that might be identified for a push-apart strategy are anchors, works by the same author or artist, long prose works, and very short poetry. Anchors are high-quality works with general appeal. Anchors placed apart from each other draw readers to various

Anchors are high-quality works with general appeal.

The cover often is where a design concept makes its first impression. Literary magazine covers are as diverse as the staffs that create them.

parts of the magazine, just as large department stores anchor a shopping mall.

Generally, pushing apart similar elements, like works by the same author or long prose works, allows each work a little bit more of its own identity. A long prose work preceded by something different, like a grouping of poems or an artwork, has a fresh identity, just like different courses in a meal. Your staff will want to consider carefully what elements of your magazine will benefit from a push-apart strategy and what elements complement each other when placed together.

A Final Note

Many artists in all art forms sequence their works and link them together with a theme or design concept. In programming a concert of symphonic music, for example, a conductor traditionally places the "heaviest" composition, the one that demands the most of the listener, second on the program. Presumably the listener is fresh and ready to listen, having heard only one other piece. That first composition, too, was placed first as the best one to make the transition from the moods and tensions of the outside world into the world of the concert hall. Conductor's notes in a concert program often discuss why the conductor has brought together certain works on the same program. Curators in museums and owners of art galleries have similar decisions to make.

Study different art forms, asking how and why diverse works have been brought together. Pay particular attention to how magazines pull various forms and content together into one whole.

Questions and Activities

1. What is a design concept?
2. As listed in this section, what are six forms a design concept might take?

3. Choose two or three commercial magazines. For each one, what are four key words that describe the look its designers have created?
4. What are three ideas you have right now for your magazine's design concept?
5. Should your staff use a continuum, sections, or push-aparts to sequence your magazine? Why? Is there some other method of sequencing your magazine that you think would work? Describe it.
6. How might the philosophy of programming an orchestra concert, as described in this section, be applied to the opening works of your literary magazine?

INTRODUCTORY AND CONCLUDING COMPONENTS

Begin to picture your magazine. Imagine holding it in your hands. Can you see the cover? Imagine opening the cover. What is on the first page? What is on the last page? Your staff will need to determine what introductory and concluding components will frame the contents of your magazine. Some components, or parts, are standard and traditional. Others are totally optional. Here is a catalogue of introductory and concluding components to consider.

INTRODUCTORY COMPONENTS

Cover (standard)
The cover of a magazine should include the name of the magazine and the volume number or year. A volume number is the year of the periodical's life. If your staff publishes more than once a year, you will want to add the issue number. The label "Volume 8, Number 3" identifies the third issue of the eighth year of publication.

Art chosen for the cover might be an artwork for its own sake, not tied to anything particular in the magazine. The cover art might be generated to illustrate the magazine's design concept. It also might be an illustration of an anchor piece within the magazine, designed to pull the reader into the magazine and toward that particular work.

Inside Front Cover (standard)
When left blank, the inside front cover acts as a spacer, focusing attention on the opening page. The effect is rather like the blackout before the opening curtain of a play. Commercial magazines, however, almost always use this space for advertising. Although often blank in a literary magazine, some short introductory components can be placed here and still allow the page to function as a spacer. The credit for art on the cover might be put here; so might a helpful definition of your magazine's name. If your staff decides to fill up more than a small percentage of the inside front cover, be sure that you still achieve a strong opening for your magazine. Avoid an unfocused or cluttered look.

Endpaper (optional)
An endpaper is technically part of a hardbound book, but this term is useful to describe the use in a literary magazine of a sheet of paper as a

> Art chosen for the cover might be an artwork for its own sake, not tied to anything particular in the magazine.

spacer immediately inside the front and back covers. This sheet has no type, although it may be a different color than the rest of the magazine's paper. It might even be printed with a repeated logo or pattern, somewhat like wallpaper or gift wrap. At the front, an endpaper frames the title page.

Title Page (standard)

An essential part of any literary magazine, the title page should include the name of the magazine, volume number or date, school, and complete mailing address. Artwork or a subtitle might be added. All information should be presented clearly and legibly. Unless preceded by other introductory material, the title page is page one of a magazine. (See Figure 4.6.)

In a short literary magazine, an entire page for the title page might be a luxury. In such a case, the title page information can be compacted into a nameplate, appearing at the top of the first page like a newspaper's name does. This frees the remainder of the page for other introductory elements. Be sure the nameplate is bold enough to do its job of announcing the beginning of the magazine. (See Figure 4.7.)

Masthead (standard)

The masthead is a listing of information about the magazine, staff, and publisher. In addition to listing staff members and their positions, you

Figure 4.6
Title Page

SIGNATURE (Sumter H.S., Sumter, SC)

Figure 4.7
Nameplate

SCIENCE, ETC. (Herndon H.S., Herndon, VA) has a nameplate instead of a title page. The space saved in the 12-page magazine allow for the table of contents.

may list appropriate administrators, advisors, or school board members who support your magazine. The masthead traditionally appears on the back of the title page or with the table of contents. Some staffs print it on the last page of the magazine. It is also possible to incorporate it on the inside front or inside back cover. (See Figure 4.7.) Other elements you might add to the masthead include:

- Basic how-tos. Offer information about how to submit works to your magazine, or how to mail order copies. You may want to include information about how works are chosen for publication, policies on works published, or the staff's goals.
- Affiliations and awards. List organizations to which your staff belongs. Include awards or honors your magazine has received from these organizations or from the community.
- Copyright and disclaimer statement. Here is where your copyright notice and disclaimer statement (as outlined under "Your Magazine, Authors, Artists, and Copyright," page 60–61) should be placed. A disclaimer identifies opinions expressed as those of the authors and artists represented, not of the magazine or school.

Table of Contents (standard)

No matter how few pages in your magazine, include a table of contents. It is a basic reader service. A table of contents—often labeled just "Contents"— should include the author or artist, title, and page number of every work in the magazine. Exceptions generally *not* included are listings for fillers—short sayings used to fill in extra space—and decorative borders. An alternative heading for the table of contents, like "Inside" or "To Be Discovered," might emphasize a magazine's design concept.

An alternative heading for the table of contents might emphasize a magazine's design concept.

Contents are organized chronologically, not alphabetically. *Chronologically* in a magazine means from first page to last. If you have section headings, include them. List artworks by artist and page number. You may want to include the title or the medium of each artwork: pen and ink, pencil, photograph, scratchboard, or whatever. Artworks are usually listed separately from literary works. Each genre of literature, too, can be categorized separately, as shown by the listing of the SEED Staff, Figure 4.8. A table of contents by genre may be incorporated whether or not the magazine is sequenced by genre and regardless of the design concept chosen. Listings are chronological under each genre.

The table of contents is traditionally the last introductory component before the first piece of literature. Short literary magazines saving space, however, might print the table of contents on the cover or title page, *Reader's Digest* style.

Frontispiece (optional)

A frontispiece is a special page facing, immediately preceding, or immediately following the title page. The frontispiece features an illustration, a quotation, or perhaps both. Nothing else appears on the page. A frontispiece capsulizes the design concept, or some aspect of it, for readers. A frontispiece does not explain anything; it evokes a mood or thought in a brief artistic or literary example. Study a variety of books for examples.

**Figure 4.8
Table of Contents Organized
by Genre**

The SEED staff (Virgil Grissom H.S., Huntsville, AL) used a pen, masks, musical notes, and a paint can to underscore their design concept,

"Tapestry." The logos are repeated throughout the magazine as end stops and incidental art. The table of contents is arranged by genre.

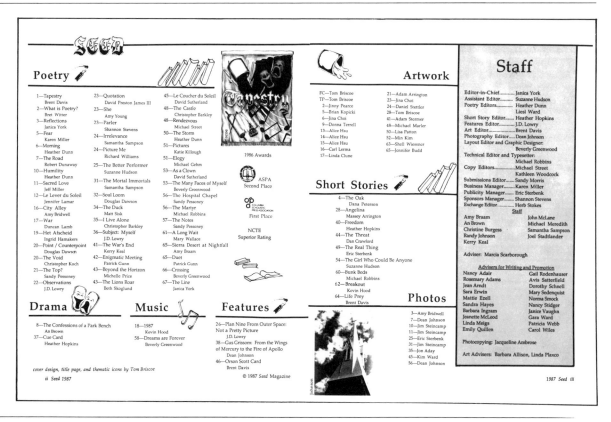

Dedication (optional)

Wanting to dedicate an issue of a magazine to a person or idea might spring from a staff's design concept or from emotional needs within the student body. As an extension of a design concept, the possibilities, from lighthearted to serious, are endless.

As a response to emotional needs of the student body, a dedication captures and verifies the strong feelings of students about a local, national, or international person or event. Be careful: Because a dedication is part of your magazine's beginning, it may, especially if prominently placed, set the tone for the entire magazine. A response to a recent, painful tragedy might best be handled as a eulogy. (See page 87.)

A dedication may be placed in any of the positions in which a frontispiece appears. A dedication also may be tucked into a page with other introductory material. The mood and purpose of your dedication should guide the staff in choosing the most appropriate place and amount of space. Be sure to write a dedication so that it can be understood by readers who did not know the person or experience the event. A dedication may be simply titled "Dedication," may appear without a heading, or may be given an inventive heading by the staff.

Editor's Note (optional)

An editor's note is a chance to talk directly to the readers about the magazine and how it came to be. An editor's note might explain the design concept and how it was chosen, report on special circumstances or changes in the magazine's production, record observations about the literature and art submitted for consideration, or offer thanks for special advice or help given.

An editor's note usually appears near the masthead. It might be titled "From the Editor" or "Editor's Note," although any title that captures the spirit of the contents would be fine. Study professional periodicals as well as other literary magazines for ideas, structure, and tone.

Teasers (optional)

Teasers are pictures or words that catch a reader's attention, draw his curiosity, and cause him to turn to a particular page in a magazine. Teasers most often appear on the cover or table of contents. A teaser might be a box, a bar, or bold type with a title (THE ONLY PRESCRIPTION/page 14), a quote ("She intended to kill the beast . . ." See page 21.), or a description (Learn how to stop lying to your best friends/page 6). A teaser might be a box with a portion of a picture appearing later in the magazine. Newspapers regularly use two or three teasers across the top of the front page. Look at magazines with a tone or design concept similar to one your magazine would like to achieve. Study the way such magazines have presented teasers for ideas that will be compatible with your magazine's look.

Other Components

Having reviewed all these introductory components, your staff may have an idea for another component. It might be a unique idea or an adaptation of something discovered in a magazine or another art form. If it helps open the magazine to readers, stimulates curiosity about the contents, or aids readers in understanding your purpose, use it.

Sample Dedications

- Because everything that goes up must come down, this issue of MOEBIUS STRIP is dedicated to the creative genius of Sir Isaac Newton.

- To all the creative minds who have lighted a small flame in a world of darkness. Joined, they are the sun.

- Jane W. Rooney grew up in Lake City. Her name has become synonymous with the spirit of our community. "T'aint really us if we really don't believe it," Mrs. Rooney would say. In elementary school, she helped us plant trees. Over the years, she has told us the history of our city, helped us understand traditions, and dreamed with us about the future. Mrs. Rooney passed away in December at the age of 93. This issue of AIN'T MISBEHAVIN' is dedicated to the generous spirit of our mayor and friend.

- Dedicated to Bill Shot, Special Olympian. You may have come in last in the long jump, Bill, but you are first in our hearts.

Advertisements (optional)

In a literary magazine, ads are often placed at the back, but before the index. When run at the back, rather than interspersed throughout the magazine, advertising pages are usually reserved just for ads. If most of the magazine is free of ads, any literature or art placed with ads in the last few pages will seem to be getting secondhand treatment.

Patrons (optional)

Soliciting for patronships was discussed in Chapter 2 (pages 26–31). If you have chosen this fundraising strategy, you must acknowledge your patrons. Acknowledge them with dignity, neatly listing their names in alphabetical order. List alphabetically within categories, if your staff has different levels for donations. Give patrons the space they deserve; do not cram a listing of patrons into a small, undesirable space. Consider including a headnote that expresses thanks and explains the important role patrons play:

> The goal of the SPECTATOR staff is to circulate the best of J.C.C. literature and art to the widest possible audience. As with any periodical, the low cover price is made possible by the support of our patrons and advertisers. The actual cost of printing this magazine is about $4.00 per copy. Our supporters make the important difference.

Theatre and musical organizations often solicit patronships. Study programs from plays and concerts for ideas for acknowledging patrons.

Thanks (optional)

Expressing thanks takes little space. It takes many people to make a literary magazine successful, and many who help you will not be named in the masthead. Think of the secretaries, faculty members, clubs, community members, and students who gave time, advice, equipment, or materials and are not acknowledged elsewhere in the magazine. Your "thank yous" may be a simple listing of names under a heading like "Thanks from the AMALGAM Staff" or "Special Thanks." You might add a short headnote expressing the importance of these people to your efforts. You may or may not want to list the person's position or specifically how each person helped. A "Thanks" listing need not be large, but should be dignified.

Colophon (optional)

A colophon acknowledges magazine design and printing as arts in themselves. A colophon describes choices such as the typefaces, paper, printing techniques, number of copies printed, and the printer's name. Publishers also use the word *colophon* to describe the decorative emblem or logo of a publication or publisher. You may want to include such a logo. A colophon may be tucked into nearly any available space in either a magazine's introductory or concluding material. Make it as long or short as space allows. The SEED Staff of Virgil I. Grissom High School, in Huntsville, Alabama, wrote:

> This edition was entirely typeset on Macintosh computers with a LaserWriter Plus printer. The Palatino type family was used for the text, captions, and headlines, ranging from 9 to 48 points.
> The paper for the cover is Linweave 80 lb., umber, with gold foil

---

Give patrons the space they deserve; do not cram a listing of patrons into a small, undesirable space.

Many who help you will not be named in the masthead.

stamping. The text is printed on Mead offset enamel 60 lb. gloss with Kohl and Madden ink.

Printing was done by Ebsco Media, of Birmingham Alabama, 1,000 copies of 72 pages plus cover.

Eulogy (optional)

A literary magazine can be part of the student body's grieving process for someone close to students who has died. As literature, a eulogy is usually a poem or an essay. It capsulizes important aspects of a person's life. Eulogies are often delivered as speeches; if one of interest to students has been made on campus or in the community, you may want to reprint it in your magazine. A eulogy may be titled "Eulogy" or "For Anna Hammerstein," or titled as any other literature is titled. A subtitle or editor's note might say, "Dedicated to Jeremy Wiggle, 1975–1992" or "*in memoriam*, Roberta McLaughlin, CU Physics Teacher." An appropriate work of art might also be dedicated to someone, in addition to, or instead of, a literary eulogy.

Symbolically, a eulogy seems to fit in as one of the last items in a magazine: It is a farewell. Consider placing it as the last work of literature, on the last page, or inside the back cover of the magazine.

Biographies of Authors and Artists (optional)

Readers often enjoy knowing about the creative minds behind creative works: their goals, favorite books and movies, hobbies, past experiences, or an interesting quote. Featuring several authors or artists in interviews could make an interesting addition to your magazine. At the back of your magazine, you may want to include a listing of all authors and artists, with a line or two about each.

Index (optional)

An index lists all works in the magazine alphabetically. You may want an index by author or title, or you may want to create separate indexes for authors, titles, and artists. An index is optional: It exists in addition to, not instead of, the table of contents. An index, however, allows you to list only major sections in the table of contents, if you'd like. (See Figure 4.5.)

An index is generally organized with two or more columns per page and uses a typeface smaller than the body copy, or text, of the magazine. An index is most accessible if it is the last item in the book, making the last pages and inside back cover logical placements.

Inside Back Cover (standard)

If left blank, the inside back cover will focus attention on whatever is on the last page. You may or may not want this effect. Other uses of this space include any of the concluding components.

Back Cover (standard)

The back cover is often left blank. Depending on your printing method, this may be a sound economic decision, since a design that wraps around from front to back cover can be quite expensive. In commercial magazines, the back cover is prime advertising space. A quote, a logo, or any number of inventive ideas might find appropriate space on the back cover.

Other Components

Your staff may have ideas and space for other concluding components. If they add to the impact of your magazine or offer a helpful service to readers, include them.

> **Featuring several authors or artists in interviews could make an interesting addition to your magazine.**

Designing a literary magazine involves creativity and concentration.

Questions and Activities

1. Make two lists: one of introductory components and one of concluding components that you think your magazine should have. Since space in a magazine is limited, be prepared to justify the value of each component.

2. Make a simple mock-up of a magazine and place in it all the components you have listed for question 1.

   To make a mock-up, fold pieces of blank paper in half and nest them together until you have about as many pages as your magazine might. Do not worry about the size of the mock-up, but try to make it about the same shape as your magazine will be.

   To place components in your mock-up, use a pencil and:

   a. Write the name of each component on the page where it will appear. Write "masthead" on the page where that will be, for example, and "table of contents" on the page or pages where that will be. Will any component stand on a page by itself? If some components will be combined with others, what components go together? Will any components take up more than one page? Mark your mock-up accordingly.

   b. Add as much detail as you can. Try to picture the space each component will take. Do you, for example, picture the masthead running across the top or bottom of a page? Or do you picture it as a column down one side of the page? Is one of these placements more appropriate for your magazine's design concept? Where on the title page, for example, do you see the address of the magazine, and how many columns would you like to see in the table of contents?

3. Compare your mock-up with other staff members'. Then, hold onto your mock-up as you read more of Chapter 4. You will be able to add more details and debate your staff's final placement of components as all of you learn more about magazine design.

DESIGNING A DOUBLE-PAGE SPREAD

Often called just a *spread*, a double-page spread is made up of two facing pages in a magazine. Double-page spreads are the basic visual unit of a magazine. Each spread is designed as a unit, not as two separate pages. This is because readers, flipping through a magazine for the first time, see spreads, not individual pages. Each spread, like the view framed in a train's window, will have an overall impact. If the impact is strong, readers will look more closely to see the details, the particular art and literature that make up the spread. If the spread is cluttered and unfocused, the impact will suffer, and readers will feel like they are passing a junkyard. Particular details will become unimportant. If the spread is bland and lacking significant detail, readers will feel like passengers traveling through thick fog, finding little reason to look out the window at all.

Your staff's goal is to put together spread after spread with strong impact, each so interesting and carefully focused that readers will want to study it further. Each spread, like scenery from the train, will flow naturally from what comes before it. This section discusses techniques for creating spreads with impact.

SPACE: THE FIRST FRONTIER

A black-and-white spread consists of black, gray, and white areas. White space is unprinted space. White space is called "white" even if a magazine is printed on colored paper. Gray space is body copy. Body copy is the small-sized type in which all the magazine's literature is typed. Gray space is called "gray" even in a magazine printed in brown ink. Black space is any titles, borders, lines, bold-faced type, photos, or artwork. Some black space is blacker than other black space.

A well-designed spread contains all three areas in balance. What is a good balance? To some degree, it depends on what design concept is guiding the magazine. The design concept "Words, words, words" might imply much gray space and minimal white space, whereas a design concept of key words including *bold* and *contrasting* might imply strong areas of white space and black space with less gray space. Some newspaper journalists say that if you drop a dollar bill on a good newspaper page, it will touch something black wherever it lands. Too much black space is not usually a problem; too much gray space or white space often is.

DOMINANCE AND FLOW

One element in each spread should dominate by size or position. The reader's eye will move first to this element, an element of black space, probably an artwork or title. Where the eye moves next on the page will depend on the organization of the other smaller, or less black, elements. Elements of the artwork itself may direct the eye, too. In a drawing of a boy, for example, the boy's eyes might look across the page to a title placed there, drawing readers' eyes to the title. The pattern of the eye's movement across or around the page is the flow. Strong spreads use dominance and flow.

Flow patterns spring from reading patterns. In the Western world, that means from left to right and from top to bottom. The dominant

Each spread, like the view framed in a train's window, will have an overall impact.

If you drop a dollar bill on a good newspaper page, it will touch something black wherever it lands.

positions in a spread, then, are left and top. Works in these positions are most likely to be seen and considered first. The least dominant positions are bottom and right. Since spreads must vary to avoid boredom, it is important to consider size as well as position in placing a dominant element. An artwork may need to be larger to dominate from the right side than it would to dominate from the left. Because of reading patterns, a bottom-right dominant element is pretty rare.

Consider a spread using two artworks with a work of literature. Both artworks are considered black space. If they are the same size, in area, even if they are different shapes, they will compete with each other for dominance. The resulting spread will probably be stagnant, without flow. The rare exception would be if one of them had much, much more black area in it than the other and could dominate, particularly if placed appropriately, simply by the amount of black area. In most cases, you would want to change the size of one of the artworks. Sizing artworks is covered in Chapter 5.

One of the two artworks could be made slightly larger and be given dominance by bleeding it off the page. Bleeds, in which an artwork or a line goes off the page in one or more directions, can strongly direct flow. Whatever bleeds, unless it is a full-page (four-way) bleed, has direction: It is coming from or going to something cut off at the edge of the page. Traditionally, bleeds were done only up and to the right, in keeping with reading patterns and a feeling of uplifting spirit. Contemporary designers, however, use bleeds in any direction. Do not bleed artworks into the gutter (the center of the spread where the two pages meet) or attempt to have artworks cross the gutter without discussing it with your printer. Never bleed two works to meet in the gutter.

Consider a spread with no artworks and three poems. The title of one of the poems will need to dominate through size or placement, and maybe through additional graphic lines or special effects. This may seem unfair to the other two poems, but use of a dominant element actually insures that more of every spread will be read. Three equally sized titles will result in a stagnant spread likely to be passed by. Dominance can be subtle; the dominant element need not blare so loudly that smaller elements are lost in the din.

MARGINS AND THE GREAT WHITE TRAP

A double-page spread has two types of margins: internal and external. Internal margins are the spaces between works, whether art or literature, on a page. Generally, internal margins should be consistent throughout a magazine. Inconsistent internal margins call attention to themselves and rob a magazine of a sense of unity. For literary-art magazines, a common internal margin is 2 picas. A pica is a printer's measurement equal to one-sixth of an inch. In literary magazines, particularly when using small pages with few items per page, internal margins are as wide as 5 picas. At the gutter, which is the vertical middle of the spread, two internal margins meet where the paper folds. A magazine with a 2-pica internal margin would have a 4-pica gutter. (See Figure 4.9.)

External margins are the spaces between works and the edge of the page. External margins do not have to be consistent; they are often ragged and vary from spread to spread. External margins will vary according to a magazine's design concept. If a design concept calls for signifi-

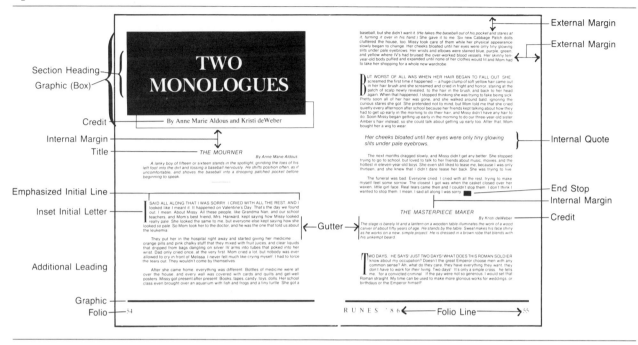

cant amounts of white space, it will be external margin space. Your printer will determine a minimum external margin that must be maintained so that print does not appear awkwardly close to the edge of the page. If your design concept calls for minimum amounts of white space, you may want spreads to be as full as possible, right up to the minimum external margin.

Margins are, of course, white space. "Trapped" white space is any white space that is wider than the internal margin and does not open to at least two edges of the paper. Avoid trapped white space. It creates an element of unpleasant inconsistency. Bounded by other elements on the page, it looks like a picture frame with no picture. Trapped white space can be used purposefully, but rarely. When used consciously, trapped white space must be planned as carefully and dramatically as a grand pause in a musical work. See Figures 4.10 and 4.11 for a "before" and "after" look at trapped white space.

> **Avoid trapped white space. It looks like a picture frame with no picture.**

Questions and Activities

1. Define *white*, *gray*, and *black space* as they apply to a literary magazine.
2. How does the way English is read affect flow and dominance in a literary magazine spread?
3. Define *internal margin*, *external margin*, and *trapped white space*.
4. Practice balancing space, controlling margins, and avoiding trapped white space by doing the following exercise:
a. Cut two, three, or four short literary works from old magazines. Try to find works that fit together by mood, subject, or theme. Choose your works from a variety of sources.

Figure 4.10
Spread with Trapped White Space

Four areas of trapped white space—at the bottom of columns 1 and 3 and the top of columns 2 and 4—dilute the impact of the design.

Figure 4.11
Spread After Trapped White Space Has Been Released

This reworking of the layout in Figure 4.10 eliminates trapped white space, makes one artwork dominant, and uses a box to control space and direct the flow.

b. In an old magazine, find an artwork or two that complement the literature you have chosen. (If your magazine will use artworks with literary works throughout your magazine, do this step. If not, go on to step *c*.)

c. On a table top, arrange your works in a pleasing pattern. Your pattern need not be one that could fit a magazine spread. Watch out: Margins are measured from the edges of the works themselves, not from the edge of the paper on which they are printed. Train your eye to see the type or illustration on the paper and to ignore the edges of paper. Squinting helps. Be sure to pick and use a dominant element. Be sure internal margins are consistent. Try several different arrangements.

d. From your staff's file of sample magazines, choose a standard size. On paper, perhaps on several sheets taped together, draw a mock-up of a spread at actual size (review Figure 4.9).

Arrange your works on the mock-up in a pattern that uses dominance and flow. Be sure internal margins are consistent. Avoid trapped white space. If you do not have enough works, cut another from an old magazine. If you have too many, drop one. Separate titles from their works and try different title placements: centered, flush left (even with the left edge of the copy), flush right (even with the right side of the copy). If you need an artwork of a different size, find another in an old magazine. Try several different arrangements.

HANDLING ARTWORKS

This section asks what role fine art and illustrations will play in your magazine. If yours is a traditional literary magazine, such art may be used only on the cover and for a few special spreads. If yours is a full-blown literary-art magazine, art will be included in nearly every spread. Which direction you choose depends on your staff's traditions and preferences. It also depends on funding available.

OPTIONS FOR INCLUDING ARTWORKS

The Cover

A wide range of artworks, available from students or produced by the staff, could make good covers. An artwork, perhaps in combination with borders, type, or other graphics, can be the key element tying together the introduction of your magazine so that there is a flow from the cover to the title page and other introductory components and on into the magazine itself. If your magazine has only one artwork, it will probably appear on the cover.

The cover is a logical place to get the most impact from the extra money or effort it will take to print in color or work with special effects like metallic inks or varnishes (glossy and flat finishes). To emphasize fine art, you might even consider a cover silk-screened, block printed, or hand-colored. Such a special cover might call for numbering the issue as lithographs are numbered (1/250, 2/250 . . . 250/250).

Galleries

A literary magazine is a journalistic form in which a work of art may appear for its own value, not as an illustration or clarification of something else. As art for art's sake, one treatment of fine works is to give them their own spreads. Either a single work is featured alone on a spread, or a grouping of artworks is featured as a spread with no literature.

Sometimes such galleries are given titles like "Gallery One," "Personal Visions," or "On the Horizon." Artists also may give titles to their works within the gallery. Readers will understand that each picture is to be seen separately, but the choice of other works around it flavors the viewing. They will know to look for connections that may be obvious (all by one artist or different views of the same subject) or quite subtle (a common theme or different uses of lighting).

A photo essay is an art form needing a gallery treatment. For it, the artist creates several photographs on a chosen subject or theme. The artist's comments about how and why she chose the subject and the purpose of the essay might be added to the gallery. (See Figure 4.12.)

The guidelines for designing galleries are the same as for designing any double-page spread, including the need for a dominant element and consistent internal margins. Additionally, you may want to include borders, lines, or shaded areas in the design of your gallery.

**Figure 4.12
Gallery Spread**

In this gallery spread from OASIS (Pepperdine University, Malibu, CA), the title is the dominant element. Flow has been subtly directed through elements of each photo, particularly the lines, direction of action, and eyes of the subjects. Consider how the flow would be affected by transposing the upper left and lower right photos.

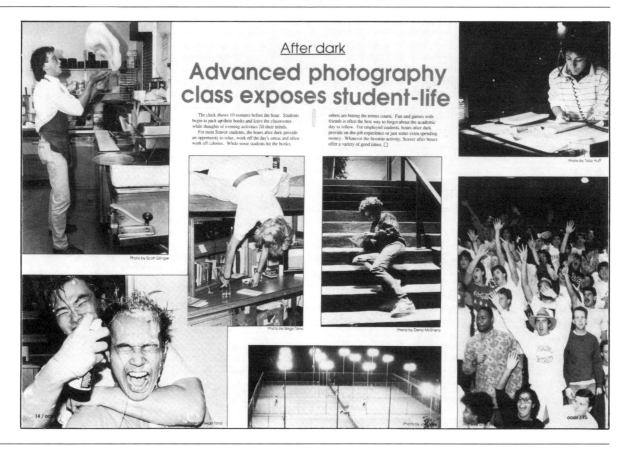

Illustrations

Suppose your instructor says, "Please read the poem on page 123 of your text," and when you flip to page 123 you see a picture of a tree. Do you assume the poem is in some way related to the tree? If you cannot see the connection as you read the poem, you may wonder, "What's with the tree? I don't understand why there's a tree." All it takes is putting one next to the other. This is called *juxtaposition*. Readers assume that items juxtaposed on a spread are connected. If they are not, the reader wastes time and thought wondering about them. If art and literature are not consistently connected, readers will not think very carefully about connections and many subtle interactions will be lost.

Does this mean that every artwork appearing on a spread with literature must illustrate something on that spread? Pretty much so. Does an illustration have to illustrate everything on the spread? It can, but it doesn't have to. A drawing of a tree, for example, might be a dominant element on a spread with three short poems and an essay dealing with different family relationships. The tree, in this case, could interact with all four works interestingly. Suppose that the four works deal with reactions to nature, but one poem specifically deals with trees. Then, the tree could illustrate that poem in particular. One way to make this point would be to box or border the poem and the tree together on a portion of the spread. Another would be to bring together the title of the poem and the tree. Both ways use juxtaposition and a graphic element (border, title) to clarify the connection. The other works on the page might be left without illustration. A smaller, secondary illustration might be brought into the spread, and well-handled titles will help each work speak for itself. Study Figures 4.18 through 4.21 for interactions of art and literature.

FINDING AND CRITIQUING ARTWORKS

It is important for your staff to know basic information about your budget and physical production before handling artworks. In Chapter 5, read "Big Decisions About Production," pages 113–19; then be sure to talk with your printer about what artworks his shop and your budget will handle.

Art for your magazine might be submitted by members of the student body, generated by staff members, or requested from non-staff members. If you have run a campaign asking for artworks to be submitted, you will need a system for handling them. You also will need safe storage space for them. You might critique artworks in much the way you critique manuscripts. A problem might be that, whereas a positive critique probably guarantees a manuscript a place in your magazine, your staff may easily end up with more accepted artworks than you have space or good use for.

If you decide it is practical to do full critiques on all submissions, you may adapt the form in Figure 4.13 to meet your needs. Before using an art critique form, your staff may want to log in artworks, number them, and use many of the procedures outlined for handling manuscripts in Chapter 3. Since an artist's name often appears right on the work, some works will not be critiqued anonymously.

Printability

Logically, a critique proceeds no further if the staff determines a work cannot be reproduced well. A work may not print well because of its large size. A beautiful 2 × 3 foot painting, for example, may not repro-

> **"What's with the tree? I don't understand why there's a tree."**

> **A large work may actually lose lines if reduced in size too much.**

Figure 4.13

UH WORDWORKS Art Critique Form

Artwork # _____

Given its size, medium, and use of color, will this work reproduce well in our magazine?   yes _____   no _____

If answer is "no" to the above, do not proceed with critique.

40-point system: 0–31 points = Do *not* use;

32–36 points = *May* be used; 37–40 points = *Should* be used.

Originality and Creativity (0–10)   _____
   Is the theme and subject of the work fresh and handled uniquely?
Composition and Formal Elements (0–10)   _____
   Is the work organized with a sense of balance and flow, purposefully
   directing the viewer's eye?
Craft (0–10)   _____
   Does the work show careful handling of the artist's chosen medium
   and effective use of appropriate techniques?
Total Effect (0–10)   _____

	Total	_____
Reason:	Extra Points (0–3)	_____
	Grand Total	_____

---

duce well at 6 × 9 inches. Complex images may lose their impact when reduced. Even more disappointing, a large work may actually lose lines if reduced in size too much. Consider that as the overall width of a painting is reduced, so, too, the individual width of lines is reduced. Some lines may become so thin they break or disappear. On the other hand, most artworks can be enlarged without problems.

A work may not print well because of its use of color, assuming that black and white is the medium of most literary magazines. Works in color may be reproduced successfully if the level of contrast is fairly high, but consider that a medium pink and a medium blue are the same shade of gray when photographed in black and white. Picture a sunset with subtle, soft colors. In black and white it will be bland and unexciting tones of gray.

Another reason a work may not reproduce is because of its medium. You may eliminate some works because you know that certain mediums will not reproduce well by your printing method. Additionally, some mediums will not stand as much reduction as others. Pencil, for example, if done with soft shading and low contrast, cannot be reduced more than about 25 percent before it starts losing lines and shading.

Troubleshoot problems with printability by showing artworks to your printer before planning their use in layouts or testing them on your equipment if you print your own. It also might be valuable to photograph a group of artworks in black and white. Seeing the photo next to the original will help train your eye. You may even want to copy artworks with a camera, return the valuable and fragile originals to the artists, and use your copies in final layouts. If your copy is good, there will be only a slight loss of quality.

Usability

Once printability has been handled, the evaluation form in Figure 4.13 has three categories for using art. If they do not fit your staff's philosophy, you may want to create categories of your own. In the first category works will *not* be used, because they do not meet the standards set. In the second category works *may* be used; they are of good quality, but use depends on space. Works in this category might be in galleries or might illustrate literature. The final category is of works that *should* be used; these are works of very high caliber. Some will work as illustrations, but otherwise effort should be made to feature them, perhaps as full spreads or on the cover.

Quality

When it comes to the bottom line, you have to be an art critic. In Chapter 3, you assessed the experiences that have prepared you to critique literature, and many of these experiences will help you critique art. Still, many staff members will not have studied art. If staff members feel unprepared, consider finding a panel of experts who will critique art for you, finding an art teacher or local artist to give the staff a crash course in art appreciation, or finding books on art appreciation from which you can read and teach each other about art.

If your staff believes that not all good artworks submitted can or will be used, then you may want to simplify your critiquing form. Consider, too, that not all art for your magazine must be chosen from submitted artworks; illustrations may be commissioned specifically for particular literature.

MATCHMAKING

The guidelines that follow can help you make successful matches between artworks and literature, whether you are matching previously submitted works to literature or working with an illustrator, which is covered in more detail on pages 98–99.

Watch Out for Distracting Details

- The photo shows a boy with curly hair, but the kid in the story has "straight, strawlike hair his mom could never tame."
- The poem mentions death but is really about the various stages of life. It is illustrated with an ominous drawing of a skull.
- The speaker of the essay is obviously male, but the illustration shows female hands reaching out.

These are examples of mismatches. Whether or not the illustration fits the feel of the story, a detail that contradicts the fact or purpose of the writing will distract or even irritate readers.

"It's All Greek to Me"

Most illustrations, for practical reasons, are representational art, that is, they have a recognizable subject. The flexibility of literary magazines opens the possibility of abstract and nonobjective art as illustrations, particularly of poetry. Abstract art is art in which the artist has abstracted—removed—some aspect of the subject for emphasis. The abstract artist eliminates details and elements and focuses on the parts of the subject that she really wants you to see and feel. Look at the works of Pablo Picasso, Georgia O'Keeffe, or Henry Moore for examples. Often the subject can only be recognized when the viewer knows the title.

When it comes to the bottom line, you have to be an art critic.

Abstract and nonobjective art offer the interesting opportunity to illustrate the mood, tone, or impact of a work.

Nonobjective art, on the other hand, has no subject. Patterns of lines, shapes, and colors take on emotions or meanings of their own without reference to any objects in the natural world. See the works of Piet Mondrian, Wassily Kandinsky, or Jackson Pollock for examples. Sometimes, both abstract and nonobjective art are called abstract art.

Literature usually has a subject. Can you imagine writing that is not about something? Since representational art usually illustrates the subject of the literature, abstract and nonobjective art offer the interesting opportunity to illustrate the mood, tone, or impact of a work, without tying the reader to the illustrator's perception of the subject. You may want to consider encouraging submissions of abstract art or contacting artists on your campus known for working in this area.

Going 3–D

If your campus has active programs in ceramics, sculpture, fiber art, jewelry, or other three-dimensional mediums, you may want to include them. Some of these may be matched with literature by subject or may be featured in gallery spreads. Like abstract art, do not overlook the possibility that a silver pin or ceramic pot may have lines and textures that will complement a literary work. A pattern of interlocking circles, for example, might comment on a play about cliques.

To use 3–D art, you will need to photograph it. If your intent is to feature the 3–D work rather than create a photograph that is an artwork in itself, you will want to photograph objectively. To do so, shoot each object by itself, close up and against a neutral background. Shoot each object several times using different camera angles and lighting effects to get the photo that best represents the qualities of the object. Because of the difficulties of storing 3–D art safely, you may want to announce a specific time when your staff will be set up to photograph 3–D works.

> **A silver pin or ceramic pot may have lines and textures that will complement a literary work.**

WORKING WITH ILLUSTRATORS

Artworks created to illustrate particular literature are not critiqued. It would be heartless to turn to an illustrator and say, "Thank you for all the time you spent creating this just for our magazine, but I'm afraid the art committee didn't give it a very good critique." To insure the best illustrations possible, choose illustrators by reviewing examples of their work or by taking recommendations.

To ensure successful illustrations, first give artists their own copies of the literary works they will be illustrating. Encourage illustrators to do preliminary sketches of several different ideas to show you, particularly so that you can ensure that the final result will reproduce well and fit all the needs of the layout in which it will be placed. Try to get artists to work with you as they go along, rather than letting them disappear for several days and return with hours invested in artworks that they consider final and in which you may discover problems.

Second, tell illustrators very specifically at what size and shape to work and in what medium. You might tell an illustrator to work at 6″ × 9″. Be sure to tell him which side is the bottom! If an illustrator is a cartoonist, you might suggest working at 150 percent the size needed. When the final work is sized, the reduction will give it a pleasing clarity and detail. If you have not yet determined exact measurements, you may be willing to work the layout around the artist's final product, sizing it to your needs.

Work closely with illustrators. Giving clear instructions and reviewing rough sketches ensures that final artworks satisfy both the artists and your magazine's needs.

Be specific about medium. "Pencil" might imply colored pencils to some, and "ink" might mean a green ballpoint that happens to be around, whereas lead pencil and black, fluid ink reproduce best. As a hint for pencil illustrators, tell them about the need for contrast and advise that they do shading in red pencil. Red becomes a high-quality gray when reproduced in black and white, and the wax content in a red pencil will reproduce much better in soft shades than the graphite in a "lead" pencil. The original will look odd, but the printed version is the one that counts.

Questions and Activities

1. What options for including art should your magazine use? Why?
2. Describe the process you feel your staff should use to critique artworks.
3. How well do you feel you and your staff are prepared to critique art? If you feel underprepared, what can you do about it?
4. Why might abstract art be particularly good for illustrating poetry? Can you imagine an example of literature without subject?

HANDLING ELEMENTS OF A DOUBLE-PAGE SPREAD

So far, discussion of designing a spread has dealt with space in a spread and the organization of its most important elements, literature and art. A spread contains more, though. Careful handling of both small and large elements is fun and will focus your magazine's look. Small details can add up to powerful impact. Use your design concept to decide how to handle many of the elements. Additionally, use your file of sample magazines to see the variety of ways these elements are han-

Figure 4.14
Serif and San Serif Typefaces

SERIF: A, a, B, b, C, c
SANS SERIF: A, a, B, b, C, c
SERIF: A, a, B, b, C, c
SANS SERIF: A, a, B, b, C, c

dled. A great idea may begin with something spotted in a favorite magazine and adapted to your needs.

This section contains many standards and rules reflecting journalists' experience and experimentation. Rule: Experimentation should not stop. So when you find yourself wanting to bend or break a standard, talk about it, sketch it out on paper, consider many options, be analytical and creative, then do what is best for you and your readers. This section discusses elements of a spread for you to consider.

STANDARD SPREAD ELEMENTS

Body Type

Body type is the style and size of type in which all material, except ads and headlines, is set. Your decision about body type will significantly impact the look and readability of your magazine. First, you will need to pick a typeface, or style. Whether your magazine will be set by a typewriter, computer printer, or professional typesetting machine, get samples of all the typefaces available to you. Each will have a name, which is actually the name of a family of type. All the samples will be either *serif* or *sans serif* (see Figure 4.14). Serif styles have extra small lines, called serifs, that project from the ends of the letters and improve readability. The paragraph you are reading now is in a serif typeface, Century Schoolbook.

Serif styles may look more old-fashioned, but tradition and research say they are the best for body type, even in a magazine striving for a contemporary look. If your magazine will be printed on a coarse paper, like newsprint, choose a typeface commonly used by newspapers, like Corona, Caslon, Baskerville, Helvetica, Bodoni, or Times Roman. If your magazine will be printed on a fine-textured or glossy paper, any serif style will reproduce well.

Choose the "normal" or Roman version of the typeface. Do not set body copy in italic, boldface, or script versions. These are designed for special uses, not for body type. In large blocks, they can be difficult to read.

Next, you will need to choose a size of type, which is measured in points. (There are 12 points in a pica.) Magazines are often set in 8-point type, but for literary magazines the norm is 9 or 10 points. Standard typewriter sizes are fine. It is standard to choose a single typeface in a single size for all body type. The exception is "fine print," like a disclaimer, index, or masthead, which might be set in 8-point type.

Serif styles may look more old-fashioned, but tradition and research say they are the best for body type.

You might also want to consider the leading of your body type. Leading is added points of space between lines. One or two points of leading generally improve readability. Consider varying leading for poetry. Figure 4.15 shows the effects of varying leading.

Columns

Columns give layouts a planned and professional look. Their use stems, once again, from readability. Readers are most comfortable with columns no less than about 1¾ inches wide (11 picas) and no more than 3½ inches wide (21 picas). Column widths may be varied throughout a magazine to avoid visual boredom. Widths generally do not vary within a selection, though; the change might distract readers. A special column width might be chosen for a feature or special section within the magazine. Study the use of columns in a variety of sources.

Laying out poetry in columns has significant advantages. Dominance and flow in spreads is much easier to establish when columns are a basic module. With varied column widths, narrower poems may be laid out in single columns and wider poems may be laid out in wider columns or in double widths of a narrower column.

Columns containing prose may be justified or unjustified. Justified columns have a straight edge on both sides. This textbook has justified columns. Unjustified (flush left or justified left) columns have a straight left edge and ragged right edge. Computers, typeset machines, and some typewriters will justify copy. Nearly any equipment will produce unjustified columns. Justified columns are seen as more traditional and unjustified as more avant-garde. Which will better fit your design concept?

When establishing column widths, be sure to establish a consistent minimum external margin for all column designs. Set the maximum column length, allowing space for the folio line and external margins. Be sure to maintain a consistent internal margin between columns (review Figure 4.9). Check with your printer to be sure her equipment will accommodate your external margins.

Titles

You will need to decide about the placement, size, and style of titles. Because titles strongly direct a magazine's look, an "anything goes" approach will lessen the visual impact of your magazine. So, decide on a careful set of rules governing titles. Common title placements are centered, flush left (even with left of copy), flush right (even with right of copy), and justified (stretched to be even with left and right of copy). Standard procedure is to decide on one placement. Decide also on a standard distance above the copy to place the titles. If you will use more than one placement, define the circumstances under which place-

> **Column widths may be varied throughout a magazine to avoid visual boredom.**

Figure 4.15
Type Set with Varied Leading

| This is 9-point type with no leading. | This is 9-point type with 1 point of leading. | This is 9-point type with 3 points of leading. |

ment will vary, for example, flush left on right-hand pages and flush right on left-hand pages.

Traditionalists will tell you that placing titles up the side of the work or below the work is strictly forbidden. Such placements are harder to do successfully. Titles so placed must be fairly bold to direct the reader, and they must be placed closer to the copy to which they belong than to any other copy on the page. Such a title must be a rather dominant element of the spread and is less likely to succeed in a complicated layout. Such title placements should be a direct extension of a magazine's design concept; do not choose them just to be novel.

Size and style of titles go hand-in-hand. A single size and style may work well for your design concept. Newspapers and magazines use headline or title schedules. A schedule offers control and variety. To build a title schedule, choose three or four sizes of type available to you, such as 24-, 36-, and 48-point.

Next, choose a family of type, say Helvetica, and choose one, two, or three members of that family: Helvetica, Helvetica Condensed, and Helvetica Light, for example. Designers may use any of the chosen family members in any of the chosen sizes. You may want to modify your title schedule for a special section. (See the sample title schedule in Figure 5.4.) Generally, do not mix families of type. Magazines often choose a serif body type and a sans serif title type.

It is possible to add an accent type, particularly to a limited schedule. An accent type is an extreme family member, such as ultra bold, or a type from another family with strong visual connections to the original family chosen. Calligraphy can be an excellent accent. Accent types must be used in a limited fashion, so that they accent the magazine, rather than coloring it.

Finally, decide whether your titles will be in

ALL CAPITAL LETTERS (CAPS)
Capital and Lowercase Letters (Caps and l.c.)
all lowercase letters (l.c.) or
Capital and Small Capital Letters (caps and s.c.)

Titles are an ideal place to use offbeat styles. Be sure, though, that they are highly legible. Never sacrifice legibility just to be different. Think twice, too, before using handwritten titles other than calligraphy. They can look amateurish and be much less legible than mechanically produced titles. Titles may be further enhanced by adding graphics, such as lines, dots, or a logo. Titles may also be combined with the art illustrating a work.

Folio Line

The folio line usually consists of the page number (the folio), name of the magazine, and date of issue. It may be at the bottom or top of the spread. It may be centered or at the outside or inside corners. It may be combined with a line or logo. It may have its own, unique typeface. Study commercial publications, your magazine file, and examples in this text to see some possibilities. A folio line can add significant personality to spreads.

The folio line's placement should be maintained consistently as a reader service. Its appearance may be modified to highlight a special section. Section headings may be added to the folio line. A folio line may occasionally be left off the page when it interferes with an artwork, such as one that bleeds. To help readers, avoid leaving off both left and right folio lines on the same spread or on spreads following each other.

The folio line begins after the table of contents and other introductory material. Page numbers are counted from the first page, usually the title page, even though the title page and frontispiece never display their numbers. If you choose to number other introductory pages, use page numbers only, not the full folio line.

The more dominant a folio line, the more it will control design of spreads. Consider a folio line with a strong line across the bottom of both left- and right-hand pages. Spreads will tend to be built using such a line as a base, since white space immediately above it can easily be trapped.

Authors' and Artists' Credits

Credits, the names of the authors and artists as they appear next to their works, should be given consistent placement as a reader service. Authors' names are easiest to locate if they become part of the title unit, placed above or below the title, left, right, or centered. Choose one placement and stick to it. Authors' credits are often about the same size as body copy and in a typeface related to the title's. Authors' credits may include the word *by*, if you choose.

Artists' credits should appear on all artworks except decorative borders. Use a credit line even when the artist's signature appears to be perfectly visible in the work itself. You may want to add the medium, the title, or the original size of the artwork to the name, for example: John Trujillo, pen and ink, 11″ × 14″. Artists' credits can be in 8-point type or smaller so that they slip into layouts without adjusting spacing.

Credits should not be confused with *captions*. A caption is an explanation of the subject and action that appears directly below or adjacent to an illustration. For artwork, such interpretations are best left to the viewer. If you have news-style photographs that directly illustrate a nonfiction essay or feature, you may want to caption those.

Artists' credits should be placed adjacent to the artwork in a consistent location, for example, directly below and even with the lower left-hand corner. Occasional adjustments may have to be made to accommodate layouts.

OPTIONAL SPREAD ELEMENTS

Initials and Internals

Several uses of emphasized type can add needed black space to your spreads and help pull readers into the literature offered.

Initial letters, words, or phrases. An *initial letter* is the first letter of a work made larger to mark the beginning. If the letter is a *rising initial letter*, it is from three to six times larger than the body type. It stands with its base even with the base of the first line of copy and sticks up above it. It may be used for poetry or prose, since it does not affect the spacing of the copy.

An *inset initial letter* is set into the upper-left corner of the copy. Its top is even with the top of the first line of copy. Space must be adjusted in the following lines by using a typing guide or pattern, so its use is primarily for prose. Inset initials, which may be any size, may be sprinkled throughout a longer prose work to mark beginnings of sections.

Avoid leaving off both left and right folio lines on the same spread or on spreads following each other.

Inset initials may be sprinkled throughout a longer prose work to mark beginnings of sections.

Figure 4.16
Initial Letters

till looking for somethin
Something unique and bi
A real adventure? Then pa
and hop on the next plane
capital of Brazil's largest state, Amazonas, and
base for exploring both the Amazon jungle,
square miles of it, and the Amazon River, the wo
You'll enjoy visiting the city itself, for in many

CHAPTER 2

Aeneas tells Dido about the Trojan horse and the destruction of Troy.

The Tyrians sat in hushed silence, all eyes directed upon Aeneas as he began to speak.

Words cannot express, oh Queen, the grief you are asking me to remember: how the Greeks overthrew Troy's great and wealthy kingdom and the sickening sights I saw. Even a warrior like Achilles or stern Ulysses could not refrain from tears as he told such a tale! However, if you wish to hear about Troy's destruction, I shall tell you, though my mind

Rising and inset initials may be boxed, use added lines, or stand alone; they may be in the style of the titles, body copy, or an entirely different typestyle. There are many ways to link initials to a design concept. Figure 4.16 shows some examples.

Initial words or phrases can also add emphasis to the beginnings of works. The first word of every work may be set in all capital letters, boldface type, or caps and small caps. Use the body copy typeface. The opening phrase of each work may be similarly treated. If you emphasize initial phrases, about half the line should be emphasized, choosing a logical unit of thought:

No: AMBROSE J. Mulligan sat thinking.
Yes: AMBROSE J. MULLIGAN sat thinking.
No: THIS MORNING ABOUT ten o'clock, the phone rang.
Yes: THIS MORNING ABOUT TEN O'CLOCK, the phone rang.

You might want to modify initials for a special section, but, otherwise, decide on one way to do them and stick to it.

Internal quotes. An internal quote is a sentence or phrase lifted from a work and reprinted in a larger or bolder typeface. The typeface should be related to the title or body copy. Internal quotes are generally placed in columns, set off from the body copy by their larger size and perhaps by a graphic line or box. Their use is primarily for prose. Internal quotes draw readers into longer works, help break up large areas of gray space, and stretch works to fill space.

Choose interesting, eye-catching lines for internal quotes. Place them at about or slightly after the place the line actually appears in the work. Study examples in this textbook and commercial examples for a wide variety of ideas.

Lines and Borders

Lines, or rules, may be etched into a mimeograph master, drawn carefully with black ink, generated by computer, or applied with commercially produced tapes. Simple as they are, lines can add dramatic emphasis to spreads. The lines themselves may be simple or highly decorative patterns. Lines can underscore a design concept.

**Internal quotes
draw readers into
longer works.**

Adding lines to the folio line or title design will create a rhythm repeated throughout the magazine. Lines may set off internal quotes with one line (top, bottom, or side), two lines (top and bottom, or any two adjacent sides), or four lines (a box). Likewise, bordering one work in a spread will isolate it, giving extra emphasis and identity, particularly if it is a smaller work likely not to be seen on a large page. Artworks, particularly ones with low contrast, can be bordered to add emphasis. A literary work may be bordered with its artwork to unify the two. Entire pages or spreads can be bordered to unify and emphasize particular contents. Unbroken four-sided bordering of whole pages, when used often, will create a conservative or traditional look.

Lines can identify special sections or special spreads. Lines or a box can identify a special component, such as profiles of authors, sprinkled throughout a magazine.

Once a box has been established, the internal margin is measured from the edges of that box. Within the box, standard rules of margins and trapped white space do not apply; type or artwork may be handled by designers as they see fit. Within the box anything goes. See the use of a box in Figure 4.18.

Within the box anything goes.

Use lines carefully and intentionally. Overuse or too complicated a line can rob spreads of focus. Choose one or two lines and use them logically. Be sure lines serve a function and extend naturally from your design concept. Study magazines and examples in this text, looking particularly for use of lines.

End Stops

An end stop provides the reader with a quick visual marker of the end of a work. It is a reassuring reader service and a chance to add a bit of black space to spreads. Generally used for prose, it might also be used for longer poems. *Time* and *Insight* use a simple black square; *Cyclist*, a small bicycle; *Reader's Digest*, a short, colored line; *Sports Illustrated*, a stylized *SI*. Choose an end stop directly related to your magazine's name or design concept; logos often make good end stops. You may or may not want to change your end stop every year.

End stops are most often placed immediately after the last word of the work or at the end of the line, flush with the column's right edge. End stops are often about as tall as capital letters in the body copy and will be easier to place if the body copy has leading.

Jumps

To jump a story is to continue it on another spread. A jump is also the part of the story so continued. Consider a one-act play that will take six pages, or three spreads, to print. "Should we run all six pages in a row?" a staff member might ask. "Should all six pages be illustrated?" For a literary-art magazine, the answer probably will be "no" to both questions. Six pages would create an awkwardly large block, possibly heavy with gray space or demanding many illustrations. A jump offers a practical alternative.

Start lengthy literary works with a two-page spread. Incorporate art to interact with the literature. Do not overfill the spread so that it becomes an intimidating block of gray space to read. At the bottom right column of the spread, put "continued on page 00," and end the work on pages reserved for jumps at the back of the magazine. At the back of the magazine, do not forget to repeat the title of the work and put "continued from page 00."

Spreads with poetry challenge designers. You may need to experiment to find the best layout.

Commercial magazines and newspapers use jumps. The technique catches readers' interest in one spread, occasionally two if they are heavily illustrated. Once readers have read two pages, they will probably make the jump and continue reading. Material jumped to the back is space-efficient, because it is not illustrated and uses no internal quotes or other graphics; it is running gray space. Jumps help control the space longer works take and minimize the problem of longer works dominating large blocks of space in the middle of a magazine.

Traditional literary magazines, not literary-art magazines, do not use jumps. Since interaction with art is not their tradition, and since making a jump interrupts slightly readers' interaction with the literature, jumps do not fit traditional literary magazine philosophy.

PROBLEMS WITH POETRY

In many literary magazines, poetry is the most common genre, comprising well over 50 percent of the content. Poetry is harder to lay out than prose for two reasons. First, poetry must, for the most part, be presented as given by the author. Words and spacing cannot be altered without altering meaning. Designers need to read carefully to discover the relationship between each poem's shape and its content—the shape of a poem should drive its layout. Second, poetry takes some pretty odd shapes sometimes. Oddly shaped poems can be both a delight and a frustration to the designer. Here are ideas for handling the peculiarities of designing for poetry.

Poetry takes some pretty odd shapes sometimes.

Ragged Left, Ragged Right, or Both
Poems can give designers headaches when trying to figure out internal margins. Poems rarely have straight edges like the columns of a newspaper article often do. Some have one ragged edge, some have two. Where, for example, are the left and right edges of this poem by Lisa Weers?

```
the red
        gold kite
                    struggled to be      free
        in the cold swirls of march sky.
```

The left edge of this poem must be a vertical line passing to the left of the *t* in *the*. The right edge will pass to the right of the *e* in *free*. In other words, words extending farthest to the left and right must determine where the left and right edges of a poem are. Top and bottom present no particular problem. Picture any poem as an image on a rectangular background.

Any white space between the left and right margins of a poem is the background of the poem. Like white background in a watercolor or rests in music, this white space is part of the author's work. It is not trapped white space. No other type should intrude into this white space, not even the poem's own title. Resist the urge to "decorate," with doodles or designs, this important white space. Let the space speak for itself.

Line Length

A poem with very long lines, or maybe just a couple of long lines sticking out, may be difficult to fit into a spread. If the pattern was carefully chosen, you will want to try to accommodate it, but the author may be perfectly willing to negotiate a change.

For lines that physically will not fit your page or column width, it is common to run over the end of the line. Runover lines are set flush with the right margin.

```
Till I scarcely more than muttered, "Other friends have flown before—
On the morrow he will leave me as my hopes have flown before."
              Then the bird said, "Nevermore."
```

becomes:

```
Till I scarcely more than muttered, "Other friends have
                                              flown before—
     On the morrow he will leave me as my hopes have
                                              flown before."
              Then the bird said, "Nevermore."
```

Edgar Allan Poe's second use of *flown* would fit on the second line, but the example makes it part of the runover to parallel the line above. True, the meaning is affected by the change in lining, but Poe's poems often must be printed with runovers. Authors will usually understand the need for such changes.

All That White Space

Despite careful plans to control and balance space, some spreads with several poems can end up with far too much white space. The body copy looks wispy on the page, the eye is drawn to irregular white spaces, and the spread has little impact. Be sure that the problem is not trapped white space, or too much external margin space. Part of the problem might even be each poem's own white space, its background. Some of the background may *look* like trapped white space. This is particularly liable to happen with groupings of very irregularly shaped poems or many short poems.

Some literary magazines avoid these problems by printing in a smaller format and putting a single literary work, no matter how

Ideas for Controlling White Space

▪ Mix genres wherever possible. Mix poetry and prose in the same spread. Avoid groupings of many very short poems. Mix poems of different lengths in the same spread (see Figure 4.1).

▪ Lay out poetry in columns. The columns will add a unity and rhythm to spreads (see Figure 4.18).

▪ Feature a grouping of short poems in a gallery of poetry (see Figure 4.19). In this treatment, the poems are set into and become part of a full-spread artwork that displays them as if they were pictures in an art gallery. For this treatment, poems are often bordered, and columns are definitely ignored.

▪ Design titles carefully to offer variety.

▪ Avoid tombstoning titles. *Tombstoning* is a newspaper term describing titles placed directly beside each other.

▪ Box or border one or more poems in the spread to define background space and give a clean edge to the poems surrounding it (see Figure 4.18).

▪ Use a special effect like a gray screen to create a textured background for one of the poems (see "Special Effects" in Chapter 5).

▪ Consider that a complicated layout may need a secondary, as well as a primary, dominant element. With many components in a spread, the designer needs to direct the eye even more carefully, from a primary element to a secondary element and into smaller parts of the pages. The most logical primary element is an artwork. A secondary element might be an artwork, unique title treatment, literature with a special border, or a special effect.

short, on each page (see Figure 4.17). Also, when a longer work runs onto a second page, there is no attempt to fill any remaining space. Artworks, if used, are on facing pages. Poetry spreads have little black, some gray, and much white. The background space of each poem always blends with the external margins. Such an approach puts heavy emphasis on the individual shape of each poem, since it basically defines the page. The effect is simple and subtle, for those who like it, unexciting and bland, for those who do not.

Figure 4.17 Spread with Only One Literary Work

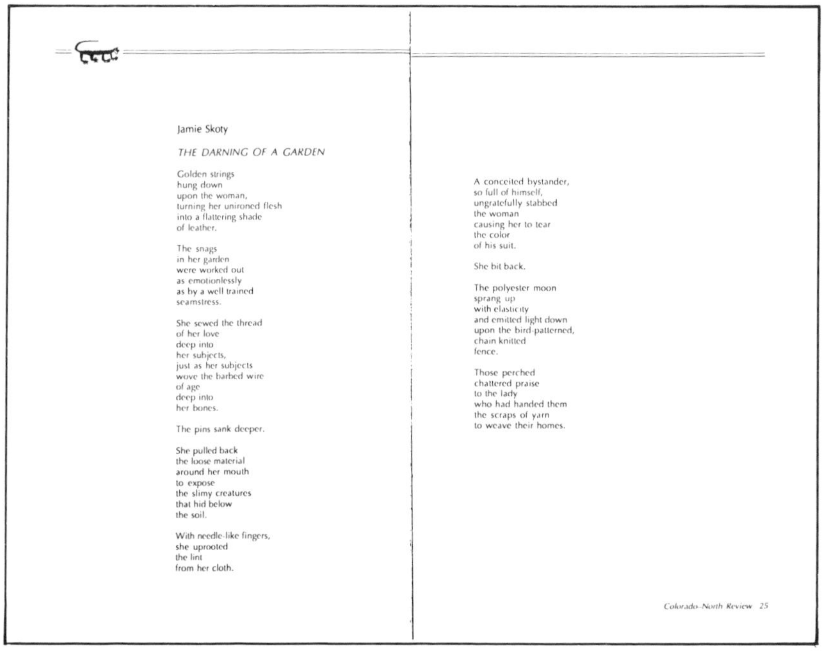

Jamie Skoty

THE DARNING OF A GARDEN

Golden strings
hung down
upon the woman,
turning her unironed flesh
into a flattering shade
of leather.

The snags
in her garden
were worked out
as emotionlessly
as by a well trained
seamstress.

She sewed the thread
of her love
deep into
her subjects,
just as her subjects
wove the barbed wire
of age
deep into
her bones.

The pins sank deeper.

She pulled back
the loose material
around her mouth
to expose
the slimy creatures
that hid below
the soil.

With needle-like fingers,
she uprooted
the lint
from her cloth.

A conceited bystander,
so full of himself,
ungratefully stabbed
the woman
causing her to tear
the color
of his suit.

She bit back.

The polyester moon
sprang up
with elasticity
and emitted light down
upon the bird-patterned,
chain knitted
fence.

Those perched
chattered praise
to the lady
who had handed them
the scraps of yarn
to weave their homes.

Colorado-North Review 25

The staff of the COLORADO-NORTH REVIEW (University of Northern Colorado, Greeley, CO) chose a traditional literary magazine layout. The folio line is at the bottom right. Each spread is enhanced by the primitive logo, which first appears as the cover design.

Questions and Activities

1. Make a list of all the elements of a spread that you think your staff should include in your next issue. For each element, write one or two sentences describing specifically how this element might look in your magazine.

2. Using pencil and paper, draw a mock-up of what a typical spread in your next issue might look like. Draw the mock-up at actual size, including as much detail as you can. Your mock-up might be for a spread of prose, poetry, or mixed genres. See Figures 4.2 and 4.3 for examples of spread mock-ups.

3. What are three pieces of advice you would give to someone about to design a spread with poetry?

4. Figures 4.18 to 4.21 are samples of spreads from different literary magazines. As you analyze each one, ask yourself these questions:
   a. What element is dominant?
   b. Is there an appropriate balance of black, white, and gray space?
   c. Where does the eye move first? Where does it move second? Does the organization of the page move the reader's eye from element to element, creating flow in the spread?
   d. What details add to the impact of the spread?
   e. Do you like the spread? Why or why not? Analyze other spreads given throughout this chapter.

**Figure 4.18
Double-Page Spread**

HARBINGER (Lakewood H.S., Lakewood, CO)

Figure 4.19
Double-Page Spread

PEGASUS (Martin County H.S., Stuart, FL)

Fantasy Feature: Reality

It would be a sin
To write my life's chronicle.

All those ages
Brimming with peoples and places
Shared with no one but me and them,
Unexplained to the naked world.

All those moments
Incomprehensible to parents, friends.
Moments lived for the sake of life,
Lived for love, for pain, for life.

All those little decisions —
The ones that really did matter.
All those mistakes —
The ones that etched my soul.

All those things —
The world couldn't handle my story.
Not, I think, many others,
Because there is too much reality.

Yes, it would be a sin
To write my life's chronicle.

— Sherrie Stubbings, '88

Even As I Stand

Even as I stand, my brother falls,
And for a moment I stop and look,
Trying to discern the small breath that means all.

His pale, ghostly face is no longer animated; his lips are
  sealed forever;
Never will his laughter ripple through the air, leaving
  smiling faces.

But he will remain never-the-less.
He will be a part of lives —
Part of the vegetables grown in his garden,
Part of the soft purple, blue, pink, and white Morning
  Glories he gazed upon in the golden-streaked dawn,
Part of the tranquil pond where he sat pondering existence,
Part of the trees, from the broad trunk to the point tip of
  each green leaf,
Part of the blood coursing through other men's veins,
Part of each man's mind (ideas never completely die),
Part of every simple home he graced with his presence,
Part of it all.

Even as I see his stiffened prostrate form,
I see his glowing pink face
Alive with life,
His hair curling freely 'round his face,
His eyes lit with understanding,
His lips crimson rose petals,
His chin proudly lifted —
Images I see even as I gaze upon a cold corpse.

Then I turn and move on,
And my brother with me.

— Meg Harris, '88

"Tree Branches"
Pencil
Tracey Jackson, '88

The Wall

He reaches out
And touches
The black granite wall,
His best friend since childhood
Now only a name among a multitude of others.
He smooths a blank piece of paper
Over the name
And shades
With charcoal
His whole life on one piece of paper.

— Shellee Newton, '87

Figure 4.20
Double-Page Spread

SANSKRIT (University of North Carolina, Charlotte, NC)

Things are Foggy all Over

by **MIKE GIGANTE**

It's times like these that I wish I was sailing again.
These city streets stink. They stink of broken dreams
and they stink of crime. Lately, they've begun to stink
of murder. That's why I carry a badge. Crunch is the name-
Cap'n Crunch, Detective, Quaker Police Department.
You may remember me from my show-biz days. I used to
plug breakfast foods until I quit a few years back. Things got
bad when they started taking out all the sugar. Some of my
pals bailed out then. It wasn't until that 100 percent bran gar-
bage came out that it really hit the fan and I called it quits.
We were all out of work but got new jobs quickly. We were
doing okay until just recently.

A few nights
back, some old pals of mine were killed. Snap,
Crackle, and Pop were found floating in a group near the edge
of the fountain in Lofat Park. The M.O. was the same as when
we found Milton the Toaster the week before. They had all
been poisoned. It was then that I realized that we weren't dealing with some strung out junkie looking for some change so
he can get some Kix. No, what we were dealing with here was
your good old-fashioned cereal killer.
I made up a list of possible suspects and hit the streets. My
old partner Sam had always said to follow your nose. This time
my nose brought me to the corner of Crunchywheat and
Nicelysweet, the corner where Honey-Nut Bee could usually
be found turning Trix. I knew Honey couldn't be the killer
because I had booked her that night. Sugar Bear, her pimp,
had come to bail her out, so he wasn't on the list either. I
went to Honey to see if she had heard anything on the streets.
She hadn't.

I didn't want to suspect Sonny, but I had no choice. Sonny
had done a tour of duty in 'Nam only to come back to find
out that he had been replaced by a younger pelican. He went
completely koo-koo for Coco Puffs and shot up a Waffle House
while singing "We Shall Overcome." They put him in a mental hospital where he's been ever since. I still held him down
as a suspect though. I've seen Sonny lock himself in steel crates
to control his fits, but when they start, there's no restraining
him. The Doctor at the hospital assured me that they were
keeping Sonny heavily sedated and that he hadn't left the
hospital at all since he got there. I was glad, the poor guy has
been through a lot.
Lucky the Leprechaun ran a numbers game in town. All the
victims were known to be gamblers, so Lucky was in contact
with them all the time. I remembered that Lucky was always
the nervous type. He claimed that some little boy and girl were
always after him. He hadn't changed much, always looking over
his shoulder. When I inquired of his whereabouts on the nights
of the murders, he claimed that he was hiding from the little
boy and girl. I decided to take him downtown.
Lucky wouldn't talk without his lawyer, so I brought Tony
the Tiger in to see if he could loosen his jaw up a little bit.
Lucky took quite a beating but still didn't seem to know
anything. We put him in a holding cell, and I went back to
my office.
While I was out asking questions, a couple of uniforms had
pulled Honey-Nut out of the fountain. She too was poisoned.
I went down to the lab where Dr. Frankenberry was already
performing the autopsy. Frankenberry always gave me the
creeps. He seemed to really like dead people.
"Find anything Frank?" I asked as I entered the lab.
"Oh, Hiya Cap'n." Frankenberry said. "I think I did."
"Well, tell me what you've got, and don't sugar-coat the
details."
"I found traces of the poison in her stomach. It was definitely
something she ate."
"Have you identified what, yet?"
"Some cereal," he said, "it's supposed to be good for you."
"Did you try it?"
"I'm not going to try it, you try it."
"I'm not going to try it." I said.
Suddenly, something clicked in my head. How could I have
forgotten about him? I told Tony to meet me at my car and
bring some back-ups.
We staked out the house. Tony covered me as I went to
the door cautiously. The house looked quiet, but I knew there
was a suprise inside. Just then, I heard something above me.
Mickey was on the roof, and he had a gun to Sugar Bear's head.
"Take another step Cap'n and it's puffed wheat for the bear."

Mikey yelled.
"Put down the gun Mikey,
we only want to ask you
some questions." I replied.
"Go to Hell, Crunch! You're not tricking me into giving up."
"We're not trying to trick you, Mikey. Tricks are for kids.
We just don't want to see anyone else hurt. Let Sugar Bear
go. We want to help you."
"You don't want to help me. You hate me. You all do. Ever
since I came on the scene, you guys have been out to get me.
You think I didn't hear you? 'Hey, let's get Mikey.'"
"We don't hate you Mikey. We like you. Don't we Tony?"
"Yeah," Tony said. "I think you're grrrreat!"
Mikey began to cry. Sugar Bear climbed down form the roof
and Tony and I went to bring Mikey down.
"Ever since Mary Lou Retton started to appear on Wheaties
boxes, I've been trying to call her." Mikey sobbed. "She won't
answer any of my calls. God, I'd like to energize her."
"C'mon Mikey, let's get out of here." I said while leading
him to the ladder. "We'll talk about it in the car."
"Are you going to take me to prison?" he asked.
"No, I think we'll probably take you to the place where Sonny
is. Would you like that, Mikey?" I asked.
Mikey liked it.

Illustration by Pam Singh

Something clicked in my head. How could I have forgotten about him? I told Tony to meet me at my car and bring some back-ups.

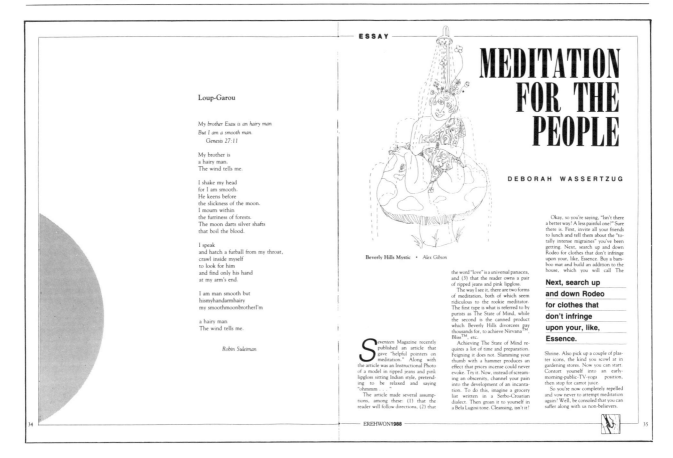

Loup-Garou

*My brother Esau is an hairy man
But I am a smooth man.*
Genesis 27:11

My brother is
a hairy man.
The wind tells me.

I shake my head
for I am smooth.
He keens before
the slickness of the moon.
I mourn within
the furriness of forests.
The moon darts silver shafts
that boil the blood.

I speak
and hatch a furball from my throat,
crawl inside myself
to look for him
and find only his hand
at my arm's end.

I am man smooth but
hismyhandarmhairy
my smoothmoonbrotherI'm

a hairy man
The wind tells me.

Robin Suleiman

ESSAY

MEDITATION FOR THE PEOPLE

DEBORAH WASSERTZUG

Beverly Hills Mystic • *Alex Gibson*

Seventeen Magazine recently published an article that gave "helpful pointers on meditation." Along with the article was an Instructional Photo of a model in ripped jeans and pink lipgloss sitting Indian style, pretending to be relaxed and saying "ohmmm . . . "

The article made several assumptions, among these: (1) that the reader will follow directions, (2) that the word "love" is a universal panacea, and (3) that the reader owns a pair of ripped jeans and pink lipgloss.

The way I see it, there are two forms of meditation, both of which seem ridiculous to the rookie meditator. The first type is what is referred to by purists as The State of Mind, while the second is the canned product which Beverly Hills divorcees pay thousands for, to achieve Nirvana™, Bliss™, etc.

Achieving The State of Mind requires a lot of time and preparation. Feigning it does not. Slamming your thumb with a hammer produces an effect that pricey incense could never evoke. Try it. Now, instead of screaming an obscenity, channel your pain into the development of an incantation. To do this, imagine a grocery list written in a Serbo-Croatian dialect. Then groan it to yourself in a Bela Lugosi tone. Cleansing, isn't it?

Okay, so you're saying, "Isn't there a better way? A less painful one?" Sure there is. First, invite all your friends to lunch and tell them about the "totally intense migraines" you've been getting. Next, search up and down Rodeo for clothes that don't infringe upon your, like, Essence. Buy a bamboo mat and build an addition to the house, which you will call The

**Next, search up
and down Rodeo
for clothes that
don't infringe
upon your, like,
Essence.**

Shrine. Also pick up a couple of plaster icons, the kind you scowl at in gardening stores. Now you can start. Contort yourself into an early-morning-public-TV-yoga position, then stop for carrot juice.

So you're now completely repelled and vow never to attempt meditation again? Well, be consoled that you can suffer along with us non-believers.

CHAPTER FIVE

PRODUCING THE MAGAZINE

NEARLY THERE

If you are approaching this chapter at the same time that you are handling manuscripts, design decisions, and a publicity campaign, you have discovered that magazine journalism is fun but demanding. Hang in there: One of the most exciting stages is yet to come. Actual production of the magazine will make your dream real. Your ideas will become visible as brainwork turns to handwork. You may even find that, through the production process, your ideas change a bit, as if they were alive and reacting to your placing them on the page. As your staff puts pages together, there may be additions or simplifications, compromises made, new ideas incorporated, and growth of other sorts. These changes are part of creativity—just stay true to the spirit of your design concept. "When the stuff comes alive and turns crazy on you, a writer had better be in pretty good shape, with good legs, and a counter-punch, and ready to fight . . . to the . . . end." (Ernest Hemingway) Well, the "stuff"—art, literature, design ideas— is about to come alive.

As discussed in Chapter 4, you will not want to begin production of your magazine until the design has been finalized. As you design your magazine, too, you will want to try out some of your ideas, and that may demand skills covered in this chapter. When you do begin production, you will have design ideas ready (good legs to stand on) and new artistic and production skills at hand (a counter-punch). You will be in pretty good shape to fight to the end; you will be nearly there.

BIG DECISIONS ABOUT PRODUCTION

Many decisions about production are important, but the decisions discussed below are "big" in their impact on the overall look of your magazine, on the design of spreads, and on your budget. These are also decisions to handle before beginning final layouts.

CHOOSING A MAGAZINE SIZE

Choosing a magazine size actually involves both size and shape. Your design concept may guide your decision here, but so may practical considerations ranging from how easy a size is to carry or hold to how a size will affect artworks and spread design. Practical printing considerations are discussed in this section.

Standard Sizes

Common magazine sizes are, in inches: $5\frac{1}{2} \times 8$ (oversized paperback), 6×9 (*Reader's Digest*), $8\frac{1}{2} \times 11$ (*Newsweek*), and 9×12 (*Life*). These standard sizes are cost-effective because they result in very little paper waste. Magazine pages are often printed on large sheets accommodating eight pages, four on the front of the sheet and four on the back. There is always waste when the large sheet is trimmed to actual page size. There is little waste for standard sizes because they are rectangles with a 3-to-5 ratio and so are the large sheets on which they are printed.

Square pages are sometimes popular but quite expensive. If a square is a 3-to-3 ratio, it wastes two-fifths of the large sheet when trimmed. Paper, like meat, is something your staff buys by weight and pays for before trimming. Discuss with your printer any nonstandard sizes you may want, and confirm what standard sizes she handles.

If you want to have bleeds in your magazine, consider this in your debate of sizes, too. Bleeds demand that pages be printed about one pica larger to be sure that the pictures bleed all the way off the edge of the page before trimming back to actual size. The bleed is created when the trimming cuts right through the printing of the picture.

If your staff will print your magazine by photocopy or mimeograph, you will have access to $8\frac{1}{2} \times 11$ sheets. Folded in half, these produce a $5\frac{1}{2} \times 8\frac{1}{2}$ magazine. $8\frac{1}{2} \times 14$ sheets can be folded to yield an interesting $7 \times 8\frac{1}{2}$ size.

Tabloids and Magtabs

A tabloid is a newspaper format with pages about $11'' \times 15''$, half the size of a full-sized newspaper. School newspapers are often in this format. This size can be successfully and inexpensively used by a literary magazine, particularly with paper quality upgraded above standard newsprint. In this format, double-page spreads are very big, so pages are often bordered and treated as separate units.

A magtab mixes elements of a magazine and a tabloid. A magtab is printed as a tabloid, but the back page becomes a magazine-style cover, so that when the tabloid is folded in half, half of the back page appears as a magazine-style front cover, the other half as the back cover. In opening the cover, readers turn the magazine and find tabloid pages inside (see Figure 5.1). The magtab allows the focused cover and compactness of a magazine with the size and economy of a tabloid.

> **Paper, like meat, is something your staff buys by weight and pays for before trimming.**

Figure 5.1
Magtab

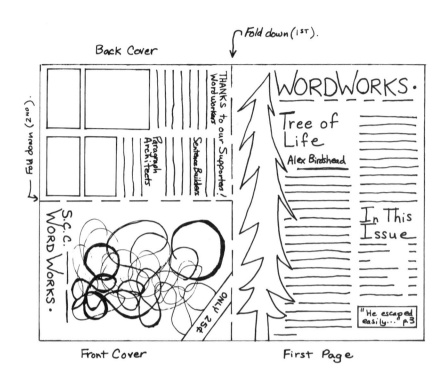

DETERMINING NUMBER OF PAGES

Figuring out exactly how many pages you will print is a push-and-pull process between how much material you think you will have to print and how much space it actually ends up taking. Cost will play its part in the process, too. You will have to decide whether to guess a little high, and risk ending up with empty pages needing to be filled, or to guess a little low, and risk ending up cutting literature, artwork, or optional components to make everything fit. In making your estimates, the editor's mock-up, discussed on pages 126–28 of this chapter, will help.

Estimating the space that each literary work will take helps too. Once you have chosen a body type, leading (space between lines), justification, and column width, you will be able to figure approximate lengths. Have your typesetter set up a column with the specifications chosen and type into it any prose copy that happens to be handy. If you are your own typesetter and do not know how to set up columns, see page 101.

With a full column in front of you, place a ruler down the side and divide the column vertically into 1-inch units. Count the number of lines for each inch in the column. All inches should contain the same number of lines, or your type has not been set regularly. With the number of lines per inch, you can measure how long any poem will be on a page, without its title or author credit. If you are going to vary leading for poetry, be sure to do this count with an appropriate column.

With the number of lines per inch, you can measure how long any poem will be on a page.

Next, with a marked column, count the number of words in each inch. Average the totals for all the inches in the column. This average is your magazine's words-per-column-inch. With this number, you can estimate the number of column inches that a short story, essay, or other prose work will take.

Your printer will probably request a number of pages divisible by eight or 16. This unit of pages is called a *signature*. Your total number of pages should include the cover if it will be of the same paper as the rest of the magazine. Luckily, your printer probably will not need to know the exact number of pages when you make your contract. Ask by what deadline you must settle on the final count.

CHOOSING A BINDING

Although it might seem like one of the very last decisions you would need to make, your choice of binding will affect the size of your magazine's gutter, which must be indicated on final layouts. Other details may be affected too, so this choice is important for proceeding with final layouts.

The most common binding for any magazine is *staples* (also called *saddle stitching* or *saddle wiring*). Two or three down the spine are cheap, inconspicuous, and functional. If you are doing your own binding, you may need to locate a long-armed stapler to reach the spine, or middle, of the magazine. If your magazine is printed as a stack of single sheets stapled through the front, making the staples conspicuous on the cover, you may want to cover them by making a spine with decorative tape (see Figure 5.2).

Your choice of binding will affect the size of your magazine's gutter.

Figure 5.2
Binding Options

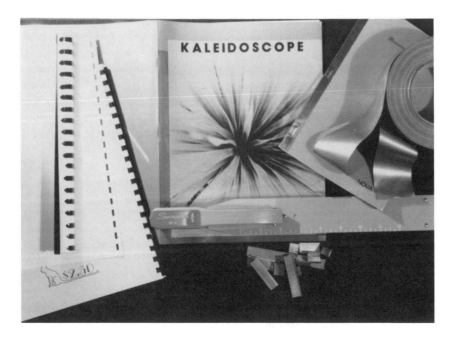

Two inexpensive binding options are combs and staples. Staples can be covered with tape for a more finished look.

Your printer may be able to offer you other alternatives. A *perfect* or *glue binding* looks like a paperback book. It has a crisp, professional look but comes with a sizeable price tag and demands a minimum number of pages to work. Also available are *comb bindings*, illustrated in Figure 5.2. The combs vary in price by size and are inserted by a comb binding punch. Other alternatives can be surveyed at office supply stores; many options designed for business documents may work well for your magazine.

CHOOSING A PAPER STOCK

> **In choosing paper for the magazine itself, consider color, weight, texture, and printability.**

Choosing a paper stock before beginning final layouts may seem unnecessary, but an early decision allows special papers to be located or ordered, and a full range of prices and bargains to be explored. Also, certain papers have qualities that should be kept in mind when doing layouts for them.

In choosing paper for the cover, you may choose a *self-cover* or a *stock cover*. A self-cover is the same paper as all the other pages of the magazine. A stock cover is of heavier, different paper that wraps around the rest of the magazine. Your printer will have a variety of cover stock, which also can be purchased at office supply stores. Wrapping paper or wallpaper can even make an interesting cover.

In choosing paper for the magazine itself, consider color, weight, texture, and printability. White or off-white is the most versatile. Colored paper stock is more likely to be used by literary magazines, since words reproduce well on any number of light colors and literary magazines use little artwork. For literary-art magazines, colored paper stock can interfere with artworks by softening contrast and altering the tone of the artist's work. For example, imagine a photo of a marble statue lighted at night: The artist intended an eerie effect, but when printed on pastel blue paper, the statue takes on qualities of a marshmallow. Sometimes magazines print one or two signatures on a different color or texture of stock. In such cases, artwork can be placed to best use the colored stock.

A paper's *weight*, or thickness, should be considered. A paper that is too thin will not be opaque: It will let light and the printing on the back of the page show through. This distracts readers and undermines the impact of spreads. A paper that is too thick can cause binding problems; too many thick sheets will not fold flat for a staple binding and will be difficult to handle.

A paper's texture and composition interact with its weight. Coated papers, which may have a gloss, semi-gloss, or flat finish, are opaque and reproduce artworks with high contrast and clarity, particularly the gloss coats. Watch out, though: Very glossy finishes can be difficult to read. On the other hand, textured papers, like stipple or laid patterns, soften contrast in artworks while adding a richness to print.

Check a variety of books, brochures, magazines, and announcements for paper that you like. Printers and office supply stores will have more samples and be able to suggest economical choices. Finally, make sure the paper you choose has printability: It must be appropriate to your printing method.

INCLUDING LINE SHOTS OR HALFTONES

Artworks to include within a magazine fall into two basic categories: ones that can be reproduced as line shots and ones that require halftones. You will need to know whether line shots or halftones are to be included when you choose a printing method and a printer. Line shots may involve no additional charge and can be incorporated in most printing processes. Halftones cost money and cannot be incorporated in some printing processes. You will need to know about other differences between them to handle final layouts.

A line shot is a reproduction with black areas and white areas, but no gray areas. Photographs should not be reproduced as line shots. Artworks for line shots reproduce well when produced in pen and ink, preferably a high-contrast black ink. This is true for most any printing method. For mimeographing, artworks must be etched onto the mimeograph stencil or electric stenciled from a pen-and-ink original.

The appearance of gray in pen and ink can be achieved through techniques like cross-hatching (see the rose in Figure 4.19) and stipling. Also, gray screen, which produces gray by the spacing of black dots on a white background, can be purchased from an art supply store and added to an ink drawing. Pencil drawings are generally not reproduced as line shots. This would apply to mediums like charcoal, too. If you want to attempt them on a photocopying machine, test them first.

Many artworks for line shots may be done at the size needed and then placed directly in the layout. Because line shots become part of the final layout, the printer does not need to handle them and there is no additional charge. A pen-and-ink artwork also can be sized for you. For a fee, a printer or other photography service can shoot a photomechanical transfer (PMT) of it at the size needed. The PMT, or stat, can then be placed in the layout. You might also use a computer scanner to size and print a line shot.

A halftone is a reproduction of an artwork with black, white, and gray areas. Photographs should be halftoned. A halftone allows reproduction of virtually any artwork, too. A printing press does not print gray; it prints black ink on white paper. A printer's halftone screen allows the illusion of gray by breaking an artwork into a pattern of dots, called Ben Day dots. Where the black dots are large and concentrated, allowing little white background, the eye sees dark gray. Where the dots are small and less concentrated, allowing more white background, the eye sees light gray. The artworks in Figures 4.1 and 4.12 are examples of halftones; look for the dots with a magnifying glass. The artwork in Figure 4.22 is a line shot; you will see no dots. Halftones do not mimeograph or photocopy with much clarity. Halftones are designed for the offset printing process.

Artworks may be sent to a photographer who, for a fee, will shoot a halftone at the size needed for your layout. The halftone may then be placed directly in the layout where it will be photographed along with the copy to make a printing plate. Computer scanners can also turn photos into halftones. For higher quality reproduction of artworks, artworks may be sent to the printer separately from the layout. The printer will photograph the art separately and bring together the photographic negatives from the copy and the artwork to make the final printing plate. This two-part process is significantly more expensive. Instructions for both methods are described in "Pasting Up the Final Pages," beginning on page 132.

A line shot is a reproduction with black areas and white areas, but no gray areas.

A halftone is a reproduction of an artwork with black, white, and gray areas.

CHOOSING A PRINTER

Big decisions are best made with the input of a printer.

If your staff already has a clear picture of what it wants in the size of the magazine, binding type, and other major elements of your coming issue, you may want to finalize your big decisions and then seek out a printer. For many staffs, however, big decisions are best made with the input of a printer, who can offer options and advice. A staff might discuss preferences, choose a printer, and then finalize the big decisions with the printer's input.

What Printers Do

For many literary magazines, the printer is the one who photographs the staff's final layouts of pages, uses the negatives to make printing plates, prints the magazine, and binds it. If you have an on-campus print shop in which your staff or other students will print your magazine, then much of the content of this chapter is information you can learn firsthand in your own shop. If your magazine will be produced on your school's photocopying or mimeograph machine, then you are your own printer.

The printer also can paste up your magazine for you. Pasting up pages involves assembling copy, titles, and art and literally pasting them to a layout sheet using rubber cement or a waxing machine. With desktop publishing capacity on a computer, much of the assembly process can be done on-screen and printed out on a single sheet of paper. Pasteups done by a printer, manually or by computer, take from your staff much of its control over design, and the service is not cheap, either. This chapter assumes that staff will choose, for both artistic and financial reasons, to paste up its own pages.

Your staff may choose to fold, collate (put each copy's pages together in order), or bind your own magazine after it is printed. This is particularly likely if your printer uses photocopying or other quick-print methods that turn out your magazine on standard-sized single sheets, like $8\frac{1}{2}'' \times 11''$. If you are lucky, your printer may allow you to be in the shop when your magazine is in production and allow you to assist with jobs like collating. Shop safety rules and union rules will dictate what you may or may not do in the shop. Get to know these rules and respect them.

Making a Decision

Get bids from the printers before making a decision about which one to use.

If you or other students are not the printers, then you might use a commercial printer, either one with a full shop that prints everything from wedding announcements to books, or a smaller shop that focuses on brochures, reports, and quick-print products. Another option is the print shops of community colleges, universities, and vocational schools, which often accommodate off-campus jobs.

If you need to choose a printer, your choice might be made because a printer is local or because a printer who supports your school offers a special deal. If you have several printers from which to choose, you will want to ask what services they offer, how fast they can print your magazine, and what deadlines you must meet. You will probably want to get bids from the printers before making a decision about which one to use. To get a bid, show each printer a copy of your last issue and ask for prices for each service you want the printer to provide. If yours is a new publication, show the printers another school's literary magazine that is like one you want to produce.

When your staff has answers to all the questions under "Big Decisions About Production," take these answers to your printer so that a contract can be worked out for the specific magazine your staff wants to produce.

Learning from a Printer

"Check with your printer" is one thought that could be repeated after nearly every section in this chapter. Checking with your printer will ensure that the shop can handle your methods of preparing layouts, can troubleshoot or offer other alternatives to control cost and quality, and can teach you what you need to know about printing.

Questions and Activities

1. A typical, double-spaced, typed page with 1-inch margins has about 250 words per page. How many column inches would this page convert to in your magazine? If you cannot yet answer this question for your magazine, answer for a magazine chosen from your staff's magazine file.
2. Explain the difference between a line shot and a halftone. Identify three examples of each in magazines from your file.
3. Which, if any, of the "Big Decisions About Production" has your staff already made? Were any of these decisions made for previous issues and need to be rethought for your current issue?
4. Which of the "Big Decisions" still need to be made by your staff? Do you have particularly strong feelings about any one of these decisions? Explain.

TURNING OUT TYPESET

With design decisions made, you are ready to choose a typesetter and begin typesetting your manuscripts for layout. The paper on which you typeset copy should be good quality, bright white paper. If you will be using a waxing machine, use a coated paper, because wax will saturate uncoated paper. An office supply store can recommend an appropriate product for your needs.

CHOOSING A TYPESETTER

Typesetting is the process of converting manuscripts to the type that will be placed in a layout and photographed to make a printing plate. Your typesetting machine might be a typewriter, computer printer, or professional typesetting machine. Your typesetter might be members of your staff, non-staff volunteers, your printer, or a professional typesetting service. Here is basic information about typesetting options.

Typewriter

A typewriter produces letter-quality typeset. It is best to use a large office machine equipped with a carbon or film ribbon. Use a new cloth ribbon if your typewriter will not accept film ribbons. Be sure to clean your machine's type. Typeset from a typewriter costs little or nothing and can be done by most staff members and non-staff volunteers.

A typewriter is the least expensive method of producing typeset.

The cost of dot-matrix and NLQ typeset is the cost of owning the computer equipment to generate it.

Dot Matrix

Dot-matrix type is produced by many computer printers and is less than letter quality. This is because dot-matrix print is made up of many small dots, sort of like a halftone, and the copy is actually dark gray, not black. If dot matrix is your typesetting option, use a new ribbon and experiment with setting your machine on boldface or double-strike. Use a larger body type in a very readable style.

Near Letter Quality

Near letter quality (NLQ) is an option on many computer printers. NLQ is a dot-matrix print, but there are more dots much closer together than simple dot matrix. NLQ printers track each line a second time, adding more dots, not simply making the first set darker. Be sure your ribbon is fresh, and you will get good quality typeset. If your school has computers but not an NLQ printer, consider saving your copy on disk, locating a business or school owning compatible computers, and printing out copy on their NLQ printer. The cost of dot-matrix and NLQ typeset is the cost of owning the computer equipment to generate it. It can be done by most staff members or non-staff volunteers.

Near Typeset Quality

Desktop publishing, which involves preparing publications with the aid of a computer, has made it possible for publications to own printers that produce copy close in quality to professional typesetting. The difference is unimportant when producing body copy, many graphics, and most titles. Laser printers, which produce near typeset quality, are major investments but give journalism staffs many creative options at little cost beyond the purchase of the machine. A local business or school may be willing to give you time on their laser printer for a fee or in exchange for advertising. You may want to investigate the many programs that exist to convert or transfer copy between differing computers. Producing near typeset quality requires special knowledge. This typesetting may be learned by staff members or the service may be purchased from a business outside the school.

Professional Typesetting

Professional typesetting machines produce beautiful copy and offer many options but at significant expense to your magazine. Also, the process of sending copy to an outside business means allowing extra time for typesetting. Costs can be minimized if you can deliver your copy on a computer disk that can be read directly by the typesetting machine, or if copy can be transferred to the typesetting machine via a computer in your school connected to a phone modem. Be aware that professional typesetters generally charge for rerunning copy you have damaged or for running corrections of errors that they did not make. Ask prospective typesetters about this fee. If possible, get bids from several professional typesetters before choosing one.

FINAL COPY FORM

Whatever method you choose to produce typeset, you will need to translate your design decisions about type into a practical instruction

> **Laser printers give journalism staffs many creative options at little cost beyond the purchase of the machine.**

Computers give literary magazine staffs a variety of options for producing typeset. With desktop publishing, you can produce pages ready for the printer.

Figure 5.3

HHS SOUNDING BOARD Final Copy Form

Manuscript # _____   Page number _____

TYPE ONLY WITH A CARBON/FILM RIBBON!

Titles:

    ALL CAPS, <u>UNDERLINED</u>

    Typeface: Dual Gothic

    Flush left, one line only

    Type title five lines above copy.

    Title _____

Author Credit:

    all l.c., flush <u>right</u>

    Type title three lines above copy.

    Author's name: _____

Body Copy:

    USE COLUMN GUIDE SHEET!

    Typeface: Prestige Elite

    Prose:

        Flush left; use five-space paragraph indent

        Initial letter: yes _____   no _____

    Poetry:

        Single space _____   Double space _____

        Flush left _____ Flush right _____Centered _____

            Indent as given by author.

        Maximum width: single column _____

                      double column _____

            Set runover lines flush right.

Artist Credit:

    Typestyle: Dual Gothic

    all l.c.

    Leave 1-inch margin around for easy handling.

    Artist's Name: _____

<u>Do not forget to initial the routing sheet.</u>

Special Instructions:

---

sheet for typesetters. Figures 5.3 and 5.4 show two sample instruction sheets, called final copy forms, to study. You may want to adapt one or the other to fit your needs.

To use a final copy form, duplicate many copies and staple one to the top of each accepted manuscript. Decide who will mark final copy forms. The visuals editor may want control of this or may delegate the task to staff members doing the layout of the work. If you are working with professional typesetters, most will not accept handwritten copy. This means an extra step typing the manuscripts and proofing them, unless you have required all submissions be typed.

In the manuscript routing system suggested in Figure 3.2, the final copy form is added at folder 9. Notice that final copy forms ask for initialing of the routing sheet, discussed on page 40. The person filling out the form will need to initial it, as will typesetters if they are staff

Figure 5.4

CC HALLEY'S COMET Final Copy Form

Manuscript # _____   Page number _____

   Titles:

caps and l.c.

Typefaces: Optima _____   Benquit Bold _____

Point size: 24-point _____   30-point _____

              36-point _____   48-point _____

Flush left _____   Justified _____

Title, 1st line: _____

Title, 2nd line (if any): _____

   Author Credit:

Typeface: Optima Oblique, caps and l.c.

Point size: 12-point

    Place flush <u>left</u>, 1 pica above copy.

Author: _____

   Artist Credit:

Typeface: Optima, caps and l.c.

Point size: 8-point

Artist: _____

   <u>Body Copy:</u>

Typeface: Benquit

Point Size: 10-point

Column Width: 13 picas

Justified _____   Flush left _____   Flush Right _____

Centered _____

Initial letter?   yes _____   no _____

Poetry: Indent as given by author; set runover lines flush right.

Prose: Use three-space paragraph indent.

    <u>Don't forget to initial the routing sheet.</u>

Special instructions:

---

members. By this time, each accepted manuscript will have an evaluation form, routing sheet, and final copy form stapled to it. The typesetter should paperclip the typeset copy to the original, and drop it in folder 11.

COLUMN GUIDES

The column guide shown in Figure 5.5 indicates the exact width and placement of columns. The box in the upper corner places an initial letter, and other details could be added. For staffs typesetting on a typewriter, such a guide may be placed in the typewriter, directly behind the paper to be typed on. For computers or typesetting machines, such a guide communicates exact details from the visuals editor to the typesetters. A desktop publishing system will generate such a guide.

Typing down the left column and then down the right column, so that the product is a finished page, is most practical for prose works. In setting works of less than a column's length, typesetters may need to know only the column width, since placement in a column may be determined later. For poetry or prose works, the designer may not want to start the work at the top of the page. To allow for this, most profes-

Figure 5.5
Column Guide

**Design capability is
the strength of
desktop publishing.**

sional typesetting machines turn out copy in long, running columns, one manuscript after another. Designers cut the copy where needed and place items in layouts where desired. This cut-and-paste procedure is discussed in detail in "Techniques for Handling Copy," page 134.

The alternative to physically cutting typeset copy is to know the final location for each work in the layout and type it there, on a typewriter or into a computer. Although this theoretically can be done on a typewriter, such design capability is the strength of desktop publishing. All type on a page—from internal quotes to body type—can be placed; areas can be identified and bordered, if desired, for artworks; and the entire page can be printed out as a single sheet.

Even with desktop publishing capabilities, your magazine may still want to use a computer primarily as a typesetting machine. Designing and printing out each page, not counting the typesetting, may take an hour or more of on-screen time. If you have only one screen, this limits the design process to one page and one person at a time. Unless you have multiple screens, then, you may want to turn out continuous columns on your computer, saving the on-screen design capabilities for special pages with special needs.

Internal Quotes
Internal quotes, used to break up large areas of running gray space, are often added to a spread after copy has been typeset, because that is when the amount of available space for them can be clearly seen. Your staff may want to devise a separate final copy form just for requesting internal quotes. Encourage designers to request several, so that they have options for placement and number to use.

CORRECTING TYPESET

Typesetters should proofread their copy as they work; in addition, a different person should carefully proof the typeset copy against the original, initialing the routing sheet to show the job has been done (see "Proofing Typeset Copy," pages 69–70).

No matter how pretty the type looks or whether it was set by an amateur or a professional, it contains errors and will need corrections. Your printing and typesetting methods will determine how you handle corrections.

If you are using offset printing, corrections may be typed for the single word or phrase that is incorrect and then the corrections can be pasted in over the errors. See pages 134–35 for instructions. If you are using photocopying or quick-print methods, test your equipment to see if this technique works.

With computer typesetting, it may be easiest, regardless of your printing method, to make corrections on-screen and reprint the manuscript. If you do, be sure to carefully label which copy is the corrected one, since they will look practically the same! Even with a computer, you may want to paste in some corrections, because some errors may not be discovered until the spread is nearly ready to go to the printer, with everything carefully and finally placed. Then, a paste-in correction will be easier than pulling up a whole section of a layout.

When using a professional typesetter, if a block of copy involves many corrections and spacing changes, you may want to mark the copy and send the entire block back to the typesetter. Be aware, though, of the charge for such a rerun if the errors were originally your staff's fault and not the typesetter's.

For paste-in corrections, you will need a form to tell your typesetters what you need. Figure 5.6 gives an example that you may adapt to fit your needs. A form like this might be posted in your work area with staff members adding to it until the sheet is full; full sheets may then be delivered to the typesetter.

> **No matter how pretty the type looks, it contains errors and will need corrections.**

Figure 5.6

CHS HARVEST Requests for Paste-in Corrections

- Unless indicated, corrections are assumed to be for body copy, which is *9-point Korinna Regular*. If the correction changes the spacing of the line, be sure to request the entire line or lines affected. Attach longer corrections on a separate sheet of paper.
- If correction is for other than body copy, write needed point size and typeface in right margin, adjacent to the quote.
- All errors are assumed to be staff errors. Mark any typesetter's errors with a large star (★) to the left of the word *correction*.
- PLEASE PRINT LEGIBLY!!

★ Correction: _slight oversight_ ○   p. _12_

Correction: _and so forth_○ _Thus it happened that_   p. _12_

Correction: _BILGEWATER_   p. _28_ — _24 pt. Korinna Bold_

Questions and Activities

1. Draft a final copy form for your staff. How and why does it differ from either of the examples given?
2. Draw a column guide for your magazine. What details might you add to it? Will your magazine require different column guides for different column widths?
3. Practice correcting typeset copy by doing this exercise with a partner:
   a. Type out a short paragraph from any page in this textbook, purposefully including several mistyped words, a word accidentally repeated (example: has has), and a punctuation error.
   b. Exchange the paragraph with your partner, indicating the textbook page on which the original can be found.
   c. Proofread your partner's paragraph against the original, mark errors using a non-photo blue pencil, and then correct them. Use the methods your staff will actually use to make corrections in your magazine.
   d. Exchange paragraphs again, so that you may check each other's work.
4. The third example on the sample corrections form (Figure 5.6) is for something other than body copy. How else is this example different?

THE EDITOR'S MOCK-UP

A mock-up records the progress of each page in a magazine.

As your magazine develops, the staff will want to monitor such decisions as where components of the introduction and conclusion have been placed, where longer prose works will start, where art galleries are planned, which pages remain unassigned, and how well title placements and other design elements flow from spread to spread. The best way to keep track of these decisions is through a *mock-up* or *dummy*. Although the entire staff may want to refer to the mock-up, it is logical to assign its care to either the visuals editor or the editor-in-chief.

A mock-up records the progress of each page in a magazine. A mock-up starts with the minimal information known when you begin to put a magazine together and accumulates more and more details as the magazine takes on its final form. At several stages, you will want to remove a page from the mock-up that represents the staff's early thinking and replace it with a page that shows all the details that have been added. Here are the stages of a mock-up and how to set them up. You may want to make changes to fit your needs.

THE BASIC BOOK

The pages of a mock-up might be taped to a wall in the staff's work area, thumbtacked to a bulletin board, or stored in a three-ring binder. Because a mock-up works somewhat like a poster or chart with replaceable parts (the spreads), use only the front sides of each sheet of paper in it. Suppose the editor of a 28-page magazine wants to begin a mock-up on the back wall of her staff's work area. Here are the steps she would take to build the basic book.

First, she takes 28 sheets of paper. The finished magazine will be 9″ × 12″, but she uses standard typing paper, because it is handy. (The basic book does not need to be actual size.) Then she adds four sheets for

The editor's mock-up keeps track of all the components in the magazine.

the cover. Next, she tapes all 32 pages to the wall, two-by-two, spread by spread, as shown in Figure 5.7.

Then she numbers the mock-up page by page. For magazines with a self-cover, the front cover is page 1; the inside front cover, page 2; and so forth. For magazines with a stock cover, the front cover is called C-1; the inside front cover, C-2; the inside back cover, C-3; and the back cover, C-4. The first page of the magazine itself will be page 1 and so forth.

Finally, on the pages of this basic book, she writes the positions of those components already decided upon. She writes, for example, *front cover* across the cover, *table of contents* where that will be, and the numbers and titles of manuscripts or art on their assigned spreads. She uses a felt-tipped marker so that these details can be seen from a distance.

This editor has a whole wall to use and, evidently, a secure area where no one will disturb the mock-up. If your magazine will have quite a few pages, you do not have a wall available, or you want to secure your mock-up and make it less visible, you may choose to thumbtack it to a bulletin board, spread by spread, so that pages can be flipped up to see the spreads underneath. A thick mock-up may need to be posted in two or three stacks or staggered down the length of the board. Mock-up pages may also be punched and stored in a three-ring binder. If using a binder, you may find it handy to paperclip or staple together the unused backs of mock-up spreads.

A mock-up on a wall allows an overview of the whole magazine in a glance, but spreads high on the wall may be difficult to see. On the other hand, a mock-up on a bulletin board or in a binder can occasionally be removed and spread out in order on the floor to get an overview. A mock-up in a binder has the advantage of *looking* more like a magazine.

Professionals often use dummy sheets—usually 8½″ × 11″ sheets, each with 16 thumbnail-sized spreads (32 pages)—instead of a basic

Figure 5.7
Mock-up in Basic Book Stage

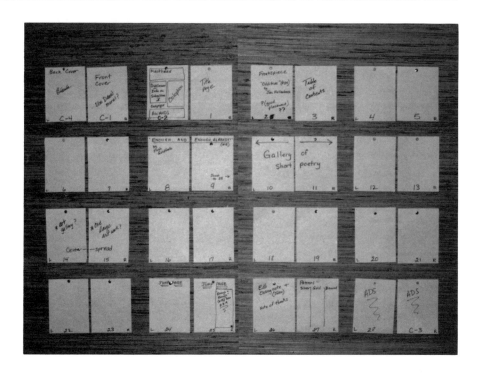

sheet for each page. These allow an entire magazine to be represented in two or three pages. Dummy sheets are certainly more compact, but they allow little space to include names of manuscripts and other details. You might want to use dummy sheets instead of basic sheets and then begin to use a wall, bulletin board, or binder to collect and organize roughs and practice pasteups.

ROUGHS

Once spreads are assigned, each designer's first step should be to do a *rough sketch*, also called a *dummy* or *preliminary*, of the basic idea in mind, showing the position of major components on the page. Use simple boxes x-ed through to indicate where artworks will go; write the artist's name in each box and a short description, like "Bill Anderson's drawing of the planets" or "I still need an illustrator for this." A column with an arrow down it shows body copy. Titles and authors' names can be written in in approximate size. (See Figure 5.8.)

A rough should be done at actual size, so that designers feel the real space available on a page. Knowing words per column inch, covered on pages 114–15, should allow fairly accurate estimates of space used by manuscripts. Once your staff has located sheets on which to do final pasteups, as described on page 132, you may want to get extra copies for roughs and practice pasteups. If extras are too expensive, use hand-drawn sheets. Blank paper placed over a final layout sheet on a light table will allow a designer to trace accurately the critical margins, gutter, and folio placement needed.

Roughs Help Editors Troubleshoot and Direct Ideas

- "Please don't use another artwork by Jordy Moshovich. He already has four planned in the magazine."
- "The way you've run the title up against the artwork is great. It would look good if Marisa used the same idea on her spread."
- "What happened to 'Agitation'? Isn't that poem supposed to be on this spread?"
- "The spreads before and after yours have full-page artworks on the left. If yours does, too, it's going to look funny."
- "I know a guy who could do a great illustration for this story."

Figure 5.8
Rough Sketch

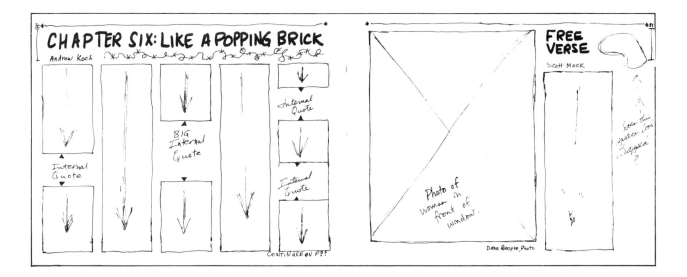

In this rough, the designer has not left
space for an initial letter and questions
the use of space in the upper right-hand
corner.

Roughs approved by the editor should be put in the mock-up. She
removes the basic sheet, discards it, and tapes the rough into its place
on the wall, first being sure that all the information written on the basic sheet—like titles, authors' names, and page numbers—has been incorporated in the rough. As the mock-up grows, more and more basic
sheets will be replaced with roughs, and you will begin to see what the
magazine really looks like.

PRACTICE PASTEUPS

If possible, photocopy your typeset copy or run a duplicate copy. Some
typesetters include this service in their bid. Typeset is valuable in time
and money and needs to be delivered to the printer free of dirt. Working with a backup copy allows designers to experiment with type placement without putting wear and tear on the final copy.

For a practice pasteup, designers place copy and titles, testing their
rough ideas against actual space available. Details like the folio line,

Figure 5.9
Practice Pasteup

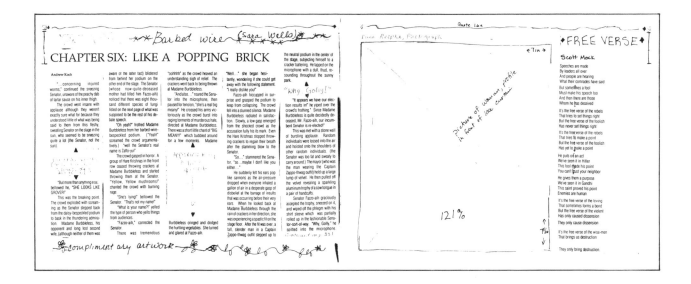

This pratice pasteup is based on the rough in Figure 5.8. Many adjustments have been made as a result of handling the copy at actual size.

graphics, and end stops may be drawn in at actual size with pencil. Copy can be held in place with cellophane tape or with removable tape. (Available from an art supply store, it allows pieces to be moved without the risk of tearing paper.) At this stage artwork is still represented by an x-ed out box. While working with copy at actual size, designers may discover any number of things they want to change from their original rough idea. (See Figure 5.9.)

From a practice pasteup, designers and editors will be able to discover a range of ideas to troubleshoot and direct:

- "I think the spread looks too full. How about if we jump about one column of copy to the back?"
- "This has 2-pica internal margins. Internal margins need to be 1 pica."
- "The folio line is 1 pica too high."
- "This looks great. More people should do titles like this."
- "All the titles are centered. That isn't what we agreed on."

Figure 5.10
Final Layout

The final layout reflects the pasteup in
Figure 5.9, with minor adjustments.

- "Good. The copy took up less room than expected, so the art-work can be bigger."

Practice pasteups approved by the editor should be placed in the mock-up. Remove the rough, discard it, and tape the practice pasteup into its place on the wall, first being sure that all the information included in the rough—like titles, credits, end stops, and page numbers—has been incorporated in the pasteup. As practice pasteups become a part of the mock-up, some spreads may still be represented by basic sheets and others by roughs. With each added practice pasteup, the mock-up will bring your magazine into sharper focus.

If practice pasteups are done accurately, it should be possible to compile the table of contents and index, if any, from them. While the practice pasteup involves a lot of trial and error, the work definitely pays off. Once the practice pasteup is completed, it can be used as the model for the final pasteup—all you need to do is duplicate the practice spread and add the artwork (see Figure 5.10). Final pasteups are also known as *final layouts*, *printer-ready pages*, or *camera-ready layouts*.

Questions and Activities

1. Suppose a staff member says to you, "Doing every spread three times is a waste. I don't see why we have to do a rough, a practice pasteup, *and* a final pasteup." How would you answer this person?
2. What format and storage method would you recommend for your staff's mock-up? Why?

PASTING UP THE FINAL PAGES

It is time to venture into the cut-and-paste process that gives shape to your magazine. This section provides instructions for pasteup, checklists of equipment and supplies, and an overview of layout techniques and ideas. Whenever possible, seek out knowledgeable students, faculty, or community members who can demonstrate pasteup skills for you.

BASIC SUPPLIES AND EQUIPMENT

Regardless of printing method, there are certain basics you will need to gather to begin pasteup. Luckily, the basics are easily affordable and fun to work with.

Layout Sheets
You will need sheets of paper with edges, margins, the gutter, columns, and folio line position marked for each spread. Such sheets come marked in non-photo or non-reproducing ink, usually blue. The entire sheet often has a non-photo grid for positioning copy. Staffs using the techniques beginning on page 139 will want to paste up their magazine on mounting boards, which are heavier layout sheets. Layout sheets or mounting boards might be available from your printer, an office supply store, or the company that prints your school yearbook.

Non-Photo Pens and Pencils
A non-photo pen uses an ink, usually blue, that will not reproduce under a printer's camera. Unfortunately, some photocopiers pick up non-photo ink; test first before photocopying posters or your magazine. Non-photo ballpoints, felt-tips, and pencils fill a variety of needs from marking guidelines to writing instructions on a layout.

Utility Knives
Utility knives (common brand: X-acto) are basic to cutting and handling copy and art. Use a slim point and be sure it is sharp. Have on hand extra blades and maybe a whetstone for sharpening.

Metal Rulers
Plastic and wood rulers will be handy for a variety of uses, but a knife blade will quickly destroy their edges. Be sure to have metal ones on hand for cutting against. A few rulers marked in points and picas will be helpful, too.

Wax or Rubber Cement
To stick copy and art to the final layout, whether in small chunks or full sheets, you will need either rubber cement or wax. Rubber cement provides a flat, permanent bond, and excess cement may be rubbed off

> Some photocopiers pick up non-photo ink; test first before photocopying posters or your magazine.

when dry. Wax may be more desirable because waxed copy may be picked up and put down on a page numerous times. Wax is applied with a waxer, which heats the wax in a reservoir and applies it on a roller. Professional typesetters will often wax copy for you.

Correction Fluid

White correction fluid, applied with a small brush from a bottle, not only corrects typewriter errors; it may be used to eliminate any unwanted marks or dirt on a layout.

Tapes

Stock in masking tape and cellophane tape for a variety of uses. Also handy are reusable layout tape, for temporarily sticking down artwork or copy, and white opaquing tape, to hide errors and define edges. Both are available from art supply stores.

Light Tables

Professional journalists use light tables in order to see through copy and other items to the non-photo marks and other reference points on a layout sheet. Basically, a light table directs light up through a layout from behind. Such tables are sold commercially or may be constructed. If your school doesn't have enough tables or enough space to store them, use windows. Windows do not work at night, of course, and in very cold weather wax near a window will not stick.

Cutting Surface

Utility knives can do major damage to desktops and counters. Be sure to use work tables with appropriate tops.

Use light tables to see through copy and other items to the non-photo marks and other reference points on a layout sheet.

> **Copy needs to be straight horizontally as well as flush against its column or some other vertical mark.**

Once copy position has been determined by your practice pasteup, the only trick to pasting it up is straightening it. Copy needs to be straight horizontally as well as flush against its column or some other vertical mark. Remember that the copy itself is to be straight, not the edge of the paper on which it is printed. Use the non-photo grid on the layout sheet as a guide for straight copy. Without a light table, a ruler placed along a line in the copy can guide placement on the grid. Given a layout without a grid, use a T-square and a triangle to place copy. Should you have access to a drafting table, use the parallel rule. Never trust your eye to tell you that copy is straight; too many factors in a layout work to throw it off.

If the demands of a layout are such that copy must be cut into several blocks to be positioned, number each block carefully as you cut it. Number in the margin of each piece with a non-photo pen, so that there is no doubt about what follows what.

With the copy straight, hold it in place by burnishing it. Place a clean sheet of paper over the copy and rub without moving the cover sheet. Be especially careful when burnishing small chunks of copy so they will not fall off. Avoid rubbing the copy itself at any time, because the oils in your hands may cause smears or spread dirt. In fact, handle final copy as little as possible; the cleaner it is when it arrives at the printer's, the better.

Corrections

Corrections of body copy or titles may be pasted in over previously laid type. Be sure to use a ruler to check alignment of the correction in the line of copy. To fit a correction into a line of type requires close trimming with a sharp—repeat *sharp*—knife. If you accidentally run the knife into the copy, nicking it, replace the copy. Use the knife blade rather than your fingers to position the corrections; the type will re-

Practice pasteup is the time to experiment with placement. If you have worked out the details in the practice pasteup, you will know exactly where each artwork and piece of copy goes in the final layout.

main cleaner. If possible, wax sheets of corrections before they are cut apart. To wax copy too small to fit through the waxer's roller, apply wax with a toothpick or small, rolled paper dipped into the reservoir. For rubber cement, apply very small amounts to corrections, since rubbing off excess cement may damage copy. Be sure the correction covers up all of the type it replaces. Burnish corrections very carefully.

For offset printing, spreads will be photographed under light so intense that shadows, such as where edges of paper meet, will be eliminated. The edges of corrections pasted in and of blocks of copy, therefore, will not be seen in the final product.

Titles

If your titles are not typeset right along with body copy, assemble or complete each title on a separate piece of paper, which can then be mounted in the layout. This works well for rub-off letters purchased at an art store or for hand-done titles. A layout is a collection point, where all the parts of the spread come together. Attempting to create a title or art directly on the layout sheet puts hours of work unnecessarily at risk.

TECHNIQUES FOR HANDLING ART

Artworks, like other components of a spread, can be pasted into the final layout. However, if your staff wants artworks handled as separate negatives for the highest possible quality, then see page 140–141 for instructions.

Sizing Artworks

Some artworks, particularly if done by an illustrator especially for your magazine, will be line shots at the appropriate size, ready to be pasted in. Many artworks, however, will fit one of these categories: the artwork is the wrong size; the artwork needs to be halftoned; or the artwork is too valuable to the artist to be pasted in. (See ''Including Line Shots or Halftones,'' page 117.) These situations all demand that the artwork be sized by the staff, then handled by a photographer, so that a final, sized copy can be pasted into the final layout. The photographer who handles this work may be your printer or a separate shop, perhaps one specializing in photo services for journalists.

Sizing artworks means dealing with simple percentages and proportions. If, for example, an artwork is at the needed size but needs halftoning, ask the photographer to shoot a halftone at 100 percent of original size. If the artwork needs to be half the size, ask for 50 percent of original size. An artwork that needs to be reproduced at twice the size would be shot at 200 percent of original size. The worksheet in Figure 5.12 gives guidelines for sizing and cropping artworks.

Bleeds

Artworks or lines that bleed must be placed in the layout so that each side that will bleed extends 1 pica, or about ¼ inch, beyond the mark for the physical edge of the page. In sizing an artwork that bleeds, this additional width or height must be calculated as part of the measurements of the desired reproduction size.

Be sure the correction covers up all of the type it replaces.

Sizing artworks means dealing with simple percentages and proportions.

Figure 5.11
Cropped Artwork

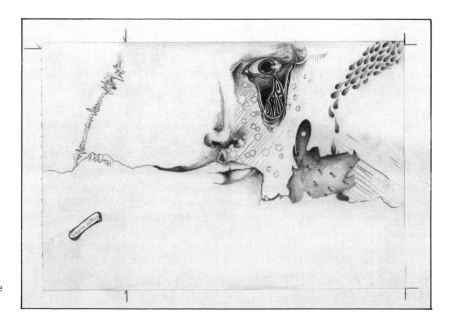

This artwork, with both vertical and horizontal cropmarks, is ready for the photographer.

Cropping Artworks

Cropping means removing unwanted space in an artwork. Whereas newspaper journalists may crop photos ruthlessly, cropping of artworks is a very different matter. An artist consciously thinks about the amount of background space or detail to include and the exact placement of details within a particular shape. These are creative decisions by the artist, and cropping could alter them significantly. Taking 2 inches off the left side of a photo, for example, might result in centering the major focus of the work, whereas the artist intended it to be placed one-third of the way across the photo. The general guideline is that cropping 10 to 15 percent of the image area to accommodate sizing needs is acceptable; any more than that should not be done without consulting the artist. The cropped area might be taken from one side, or some from each side. Be sensitive to individual works; some can be cropped, whereas others are so carefully framed that cropping would be a poor decision. (See Figure 5.11.)

Before learning when and how to crop, realize that cropping is something done by a camera, not something done physically to an artwork. Never cut or permanently mark an original artwork or the only usable reproduction of it! There are two reasons for this. First, an artwork is of value other than as an illustration. Artworks should be returned to artists without damage. Second, cuts and permanent marks represent decisions that cannot be changed. This means that physical cropping should not be done even to originals owned by a literary magazine. Should a designer get a better idea or realize he calculated incorrectly, he cannot reverse his decision. If you have reason to cut a work, be sure to have a backup available.

Cropping is done by making marks in the margin of the work. Use the white margin of a photo or the mat of a drawing. If there is no usable margin, as on a painting, mark carefully on the edge or back near the edge. Sometimes it is possible to mount the artwork on another piece of paper. Mark a quarter-inch line with pencil or something else erasable. Art stores can provide self-adhesive bull's-eyes appropriate for marking many works. The mark needs to be clear and placed exactly. Instructions added later will tell the photographer to look for the marks. To crop vertically, make two vertical marks parallel to each other, top and bottom. To crop horizontally, make two horizontal marks parallel to each other, left and right. Photographers will know not to print the area to the outside of your marks. If the edges of an artwork are not the obvious edges of the paper, indicate them with crop marks.

The worksheet in Figure 5.13 will help you through the process of sizing and cropping artworks. It requires use of a proportion wheel, an inexpensive tool available from an art supply store (see Figure 5.12). The sample in the worksheet starts with desired width because more often width, not height, is the critical measurement. The example given is for a 5″ × 8″ photo that the designer wants to reproduce at 3½ inches wide.

Labeling Artworks

Once you have sized and cropped artworks, you will need to give the photographer instructions for handling each one. Writing directly on the back of an artwork can make quite a mess if calculations are changed, and some inks may rub off or come through. To protect artworks, use a small form that can be taped to the back. It will offer information in a standard format, easily located by the photographer. Figure 5.14 shows such a form, which you may want to show to your photographer before using and modify to fit your needs.

Figure 5.12
Proportion Wheel

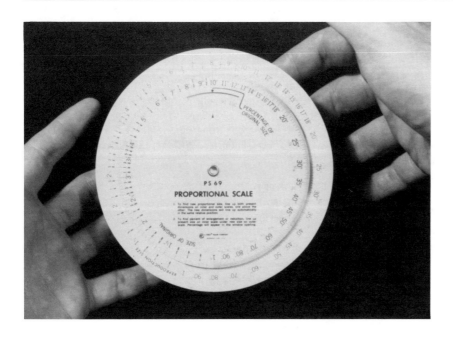

A proportion wheel can speed sizing of artworks.

Figure 5.12

HSU VANTAGE POINT Worksheet for Sizing
and Cropping Artworks

Calculate all measurements to the nearest ¹/₈-inch.

1. What are the measurements of the original artwork?
    ORIGINAL WIDTH: __*5"*__
    ORIGINAL HEIGHT: __*8"*__
2. What is the DESIRED WIDTH of the reproduction? W: __*3½"*__
3. What percentage is this DESIRED WIDTH of the ORIGINAL WIDTH?
    a. On the proportion wheel, match the ORIGINAL WIDTH (inner wheel) and the DESIRED WIDTH (outer wheel).
    b. Read percent from the wheel's window: __*70%*__ (TEST %)
    Round *up* if between percentages.
4. If I use this percent, how *tall* will the artwork be?
    a. Hold proportion wheel firmly on the TEST %.
    b. Find ORIGINAL HEIGHT on the inner wheel.
    c. Across from the ORIGINAL HEIGHT, read the number on the outer wheel. This is the REPRO. HEIGHT: __*5⅝"*__
5. Is this height OK?   yes   (no)
    a. If yes, go to step 8.
    b. If no, go to step 6 or 7, whichever applies.
6. What options do I have if the height is TOO TALL?
    a. Choose a narrower DESIRED WIDTH and return to step 2.
    b. Crop the height of the original.
        (1) The REPRO. HEIGHT is __*⅝"*__ too tall; I would like the repro to be only __*5"*__ (DESIRED HEIGHT) tall.
        (2) Find the DESIRED HEIGHT on the outer wheel. Be sure the window shows the TEST % (from step 3.b.).
        (3) Across from the DESIRED HEIGHT (outer wheel), read the possible CROPPED ORIGINAL HEIGHT (inner wheel): __*7⅛"*__
        (4) To find the amount I need to crop:

__*8"*__	−	__*7⅛"*__	=	__*⅞"*__
(ORIGINAL HEIGHT)		(CROPPED ORIGINAL HEIGHT)		(AMOUNT TO CROP)

7. What options do I have if the height is *too short*?
    a. Choose a wider DESIRED WIDTH and return to step 2.
    b. Crop the width of the original.
        (1) The REPRO. HEIGHT is _____ too short; I would like it to be _____ (DESIRED HEIGHT) tall.
        (2) Find the DESIRED HEIGHT (outer wheel).
        (3) Match it with the ORIGINAL HEIGHT (inner wheel). To make the repro as tall as I want, the original must be shot at _____% (NEW % from window).
        (4) Be sure the window is on the NEW %. Across from the original DESIRED WIDTH (outer wheel), read the possible CROPPED ORIGINAL WIDTH (inner wheel): _____
        (5) To find the amount I need to crop:

_____	−	_____	=	_____
(ORIGINAL HEIGHT)		(CROPPED ORIGINAL HEIGHT)		(AMOUNT TO CROP)

        (6) Go to step 8.
8. FINAL RESULTS: The artwork will be produced at __*70*__% of original size.
    My original (cropped if necessary) is __*5"*__ by __*7⅛"*__. It will reproduce at __*3½"*__ by __*5"*__.

Figure 5.14
Label for Artworks to Be
Photographed

> **CCC ARTISAN**
>
> Page # _____
> Halftone?   or   Line shot?
> Shoot at _____% of original size
> Observe crop marks?   Yes   None
> Other instructions (bleeds, etc.):

Questions and Activities

1. Make a supply list for your magazine. How many of each item will you need? Which of the listed items are on hand? Which might you need to purchase? Where might you purchase them, and who will do the shopping? How might your staff finance all the purchases you have in mind?

2. Suppose it is late afternoon and you are trying to finish pasting up a layout of a short story. You still have many blocks of copy to place and straighten. Suddenly you hear, "I'm not busy; can I help someone before I leave?" It is a member of the publicity committee who has never worked on a layout. What instructions would you give this helpful person to aid you in pasting up the body copy of the story?

3. Choose two or three artworks from submissions to your magazine, available magazines, or any other convenient source. For each one, ask:
   a. If needed, could this artwork be cropped? Could it be cropped horizontally? Vertically? How much?
   b. Could this work, to your eye, *benefit* from cropping?

4. Suppose you have located a $30'' \times 18''$ acrylic painting to use for your magazine's center spread. The center spread must be $15'' \times 9\frac{1}{2}''$. Size the painting, determining the percentage of reduction and whether cropping would be required. If you do not have access to a proportion wheel, use a calculator.

ICING THE CAKE

The techniques and special effects outlined in this section go beyond the basics, and one of them might give just the touch you want on a few special spreads. Some of these techniques require supplies beyond the basics listed earlier (page 132), so you may want to add a few items to your shopping list.

GRAY SCREENS

Screens, mentioned on page 117, are of three types: peel-off, computer-generated, or professional. One of these types probably can be a workable and inexpensive addition to your magazine. Art stores carry peel-off screens in a variety of densities. They apply easily by peeling off the backing and smoothing them onto a page. They may be used to add gray to a line shot or shadow to any area of a spread. Tapes of gray screen lines and borders are also available. Do not attempt to apply this sort of screen over type; it will distort. To apply, remove the backing and gently apply the screen to the area overlapping the actual edges desired. Then, using a knife, cut the excess away and burnish the final screen to eliminate air bubbles. Do not overlap pieces of screen; the mismatch of dots will show.

Computer-generated screens can be printed by a laser printer in a variety of densities. A sheet of screen can be used like the peel-off variety for art or page design with the same dos and don'ts. Attach pieces with wax or rubber cement. Additionally, a desktop publishing system can print screens behind type so that a work may be boxed in gray. Desktop systems can also produce lines or titles in gray screen. See Figure 2.5, in which the train tunnel in the folio line uses a gray screen. This one was computer-generated, but a peel-off screen could have added the same effect.

Professional printer's screens are often so fine that the dots are hard to detect. When printers insert screens for you, the staff indicates screen placement in art or under copy with written instructions on the pasteup and sometimes by using amberlith, discussed on page 143. There will be a charge for each screen placed.

HANDLING ART SEPARATELY

For the highest quality art reproduction, a printer handles each artwork and the spread into which it fits as two separate negatives. It works this way: Designers size and crop art as usual, but instead of requesting a halftone or line shot and placing it in the final layout, they send the labeled artwork directly to the printer. Where the artwork would have appeared in the spread, the designer places a square of black construction paper. When the printer makes a negative of the spread, all black areas will be clear. The clear square created by the black construction paper is called a window. The printer makes a separate negative of the artwork and brings this negative up into the window. The advantages to this process are high quality art reproduction and access to many special effects. The disadvantages are additional cost and not being able to see the artwork at size and in place before printing.

If you decide to take this route, you will need to label artwork a bit differently, since the printer, not the staff, will be doing final placement of artwork. You may want to adapt the label in Figure 5.15 to your and your printer's needs. When using such a form, attach it to the back so the arrows point to the top of the artwork. "Which way's up" is not always obvious in fine art, and printers work quickly. Also, if there is more than one artwork on a page, give each a letter as indicated, both on the label and the pasteup. Finally, and *very* importantly, in figuring percentages, discuss with your printer adding 1 or 2 percent to your calculations. This will allow for rounding off eighth-inches and avoid the possibility that the art will be too small for the window, which will cause your printer headaches.

Rather than black construction paper, you might choose to make windows with rubylith (common brandname: Zipatone). It is an art-store product with a peel-off back, applied like gray screen (see above). Its advantages are a cleaner edge and more control over cutting ir-

Figure 5.15
Label for Artworks Going
Directly to Printer

```
↑ TOP ↑ TOP ↑ TOP ↑ TOP ↑ TOP ↑ TOP ↑ TOP ↑

                        JHS MIRROR IMAGE

Page # _____     Position: A B C D   (Circle one.)
Shoot at _____ % of original size.
Line shot?   or   Halftone?
Observe crop marks:   yes   none
Other instructions (bleeds, screens, etc.):
```

regularly shaped windows. Because of its photographic qualities, it is also more likely to produce a truly clear window than construction paper. You need to be aware that in cutting a window you are not just telling the printer where to put the artwork, you are really forming the window. If a window's edges are ragged, the edges of the artwork will be, too.

Desktop publishing systems will produce black areas suitable for windows, but if printed out on a laser printer, they will not be clear enough. Such computer-produced windows, and presumably the layouts of which they are a part, would need to be taken to a printer or service bureau that could print them out on a photo image setter.

If a window's edges are ragged, the edges of the artwork will be, too.

Special Effects

With artworks handled separately, the following special effects become possible. To do them well, as well as to cut accurate windows, use mounting boards for pasteups, rather than lightweight layout sheets. Ask your printer for a schedule of charges for these effects.

Flop the negative. To direct flow in a spread, a figure in an artwork might better be facing left than right, or vice-versa. Ask the printer to flop the negative, and when it is brought up into the window it will simply be turned over, reversing left and right. Ask the artist's permission first. Do *not* ask to reverse the negative; this means something entirely different.

Double burn. The printer can bring two negatives together and print them as one, sort of like a double exposure (see Figure 5.16). This allows an image area to be printed under copy. To keep the art from obliterating the copy, it is often necessary to "screen back" the art, so that it appears as a lighter gray under the copy.

To set up a double burn, make a window for the art, then hinge a sheet of paper to the top of the mounting board so that it comes down over the window. Mount copy on the overlay in the position you want. Make sure the hinge is sturdy for exact placement. On the overlay (in non-photo!) write "double burn." On the art label, write "Shoot art at 20 percent screen and double burn."

Reverse double burn. If an artwork has solid areas of black within it, it can be dramatic to print a title or short work in white type on black.

Figure 5.16
Double Burn

To do this, set up a double burn, and on the overlay, which has the copy, write "Reverse double burn" or "Reverse out white." (Check preferred term with your printer.) Repeat this instruction on the art label. To place type accurately, you may need to use a proportion wheel to size and locate where the black area will appear in the window. Any part of a page, such as a box, can be printed in black with reversed type by using written instructions or amberlith (see page 143).

WORKING WITH COLOR

The medium of a painting is oil or water; the medium of literature is words. Since words always come in black and white, some would say that including color in a literary magazine significantly alters the balance between art and literature. Many literary magazines print in black and white not only because of its lower cost, but with the conviction that black-and-white mediums more appropriately complement literature. Also, black-and-white mediums reveal the essential elements of line, pattern, shape, texture, and contrast.

Other magazine staffs choose color whenever they can afford it, believing that a black-and-white publication does not have much impact for people accustomed to color in their environment. Color has emotional impact, these staffs would say, and that is what literature is about. As with any other design element, the use of color should be a natural extension of a staff's design concept.

The philosophical debate aside, what about the cost of color? When a printer runs a sheet of paper through a press, it prints a single color. To produce a full-color page, that page must be run through the press four times: once each to print black, yellow, blue, and red. All other colors are the result of the layering of the three primary colors. The press must be re-inked each time and a different plate used. Full-color, then, costs at least four times one color; and two colors, twice as much.

Use of a second color can add some splash at reasonable cost. A second color is a color chosen by the staff from a printer's color index. This color might be used to highlight details in a spread, such as folios, titles, a particular poem, or lines, or to highlight any detail in an artwork. The purchase of a second color includes all possible screened percentages. A red, for example, could be used from 100 percent (red) to 10 percent (pink). When screened, the color may be used to tint areas of a spread or art.

The printed units of a magazine are the cover, a signature, or a flat. Since each of these goes through the press as a unit, consolidating color in a particular unit will be less expensive. Your staff may want to ask for a bid that includes adding a second color or full color to the cover. Watch out in the case of the cover: A negative big enough to cover C-1 and C-4 is expensive. You might also pick a particular signature or flat for color. If you decide on a unit for color treatment, be sure to include this information on the appropriate pages in the editor's mock-up.

To set up color layouts, talk carefully with your printer. The pasteups themselves are often much the same as for black and white. Some printers will want you to go over the pasteup with them, giving verbal instructions about color treatment. Others, particularly for a second color on tabloids, will ask you to attach a lightweight paper overlay on which you trace with pencil the area for color. Still others will ask for an amberlith overlay.

Amberlith is an art-store product consisting of translucent amber plastic mounted on a durable clear film. Its purpose is to identify an area of a layout for special treatment, such as gray screen or a second color. To use it, hinge amberlith to the top of the mounting board so that it covers the special part of the layout, and, using a sharp knife, cut away and peel off all the amber except over the special area. The clear film mount will withstand a knife blade and protect the area over which you are cutting. Like rubylith, the amberlith overlay is not simply an indicator to the printer; it will be handled photographically, and the quality of the edges of the special area will be only as accurate as the overlay.

GOODIES AND GIMMICKS

New tools, supplies, techniques, and special effects become available every day. Die cuts (cutting a hole in a page to reveal part of an image on the next page), embossing (raising the surface of the page), and spot varnishing (putting a glossy finish on part of a page) are just a few of the ideas that come and go and come around again with a twist. Some will be expensive and others quite affordable; some will require special skills to handle and others will be easy to paste up. Computers offer another whole range of possibilities in typography and graphic effects. As a periodical, a magazine should reflect its time period, and using the latest goodies and gimmicks might be one way your staff chooses to express itself as a product of today.

Questions and Activities

1. In your staff's magazine file, find two examples of each of these techniques: use of a gray screen, a double burn, addition of a second color, use of full color.
2. Given your magazine's printing method, philosophy, and finances, which techniques discussed here are available to your

Use of a second color can add some splash at reasonable cost.

A magazine should reflect its time period.

staff? Are there any "goodies and gimmicks" mentioned here, or that you have seen elsewhere, that you think your staff should explore?

3. Review the supply list you made after reading "Pasting Up the Final Pages." Are there any supplies you would like to add for pasting up special effects discussed in this section?

FINAL CHECKPOINTS

Fine! It is a musical term from Italian meaning "the end" and an English word meaning "of superior quality." Just reaching the end feels pretty fine in itself. What is left to do is cover a few checkpoints and launch a sales or distribution campaign. May that product be truly fine for you and your readers. Here are four final points to consider.

FINAL CHECKLIST

It is not what is *wrong* that is most likely to be overlooked, but what is *not there at all.*

When spreads are done and ready to be printed, you face one last moment of decision as you stare at each finished spread and ask, "Is it done? What have we missed? Is there an error staring right at me that I'm not seeing? Is it really ready to go?" A final pasteup has been described as a collection point where all the parts of a spread come together. The number of items to check in a completed spread is too many to trust to memory. Besides, you are probably tired and still under deadline pressure. At this point, you may find it helpful to make a checklist for designers and editors to use systematically in the final review of pages.

A final checklist should include every detail that might appear on the spread. Ironically, it is not what is *wrong* that is most likely to be overlooked, but what is *not there at all*: an artist's credit, the page number, maybe the "continued on page . . ." for a jump. Designers checked their copy when they pasted it into spreads; at this time editors should check copy in the final layout against the author's original. A paragraph out of order, a line accidentally sliced from a poem in adjusting spacing—these are likely errors when the focus of creativity shifts naturally from manuscripts to layouts.

In the checklist, include checking copy for straightness and corrections, exact placement of titles and credits, end stops, repeated graphic elements, placement and completeness of the folio line, labeling of artworks, borders, and everything else the staff can think of. Go down this list systematically for the final check of each spread.

PROOF POSITIVE

A proof is a last chance to look at the magazine before it is printed.

It might be called a *proof*, a *silver print*, a *blueline*, or something else. What it is is a last chance to look at the magazine before it is printed, complete with artwork and cropped pages. Its purpose is for the printer to ensure that he has interpreted instructions correctly so that the magazine will look as expected. Unfortunately, its purpose is not for you to find any last-minute errors. At this point you will be charged for most changes, called author's alterations, because negatives have

A careful check at the proof stage ensures that your magazine is as close to perfect as possible.

been shot and plates made. The printer, of course, will change anything that is the error of his shop.

In the excitement of almost seeing the final product, do not forget to be accurate and complete in checking the proof. Editors should review the entire magazine carefully, with a checklist in hand. If possible, each designer should check the spreads she designed and pasted up. Common errors to locate in a proof are artworks in the wrong location or wrong side up, type damaged in handling, corrections or small pieces of type that have fallen off, pages not in the right order, instructions for screens or other special effects that have been misinterpreted, and bits of dirt or fluff that were not cleared from the negative.

ERRATA

No matter how carefully you proofed and checked pages before deadline, no matter how carefully you reviewed the proof, your magazine will not be totally error-free. The remaining errors should be small, but there is the chance that you will find a major error in your magazine after you have received all the printed copies to be sold or distributed. In literary works, errors in writing or printing are traditionally called *errata*, from a Latin word meaning *wandered*, *erred*, or *strayed*. What do you do with errata?

To begin with, deal only with errata that can be described as major errors. What is a "major error"? One that significantly affects the dignity of your authors and artists or one that significantly affects your readers' understanding and enjoyment. Examples would be attributing a work to the wrong author or artist, omitting a line or more that makes an entire work hard to understand, or overlooking a typo that changes the author's intent.

Omissions or typos, particularly misspelled names, are frustrating, but they are a part of journalism. Do not feel guilty because you are not

What is a "major error"?

Figure 5.17
Next Issue Correction

> *Correction*
>
> "Candor," on page 10 of our January issue, is by Steve Smith. The AMBIGUITY Staff regrets that we attributed this poem to the wrong author.

perfect. Consider carefully whether the error is more than a minor irritation. If it is a major error, how do you correct it? There are two traditional options.

Next Issue Correction

Periodicals have the option of offering a correction in the next issue printed. If your magazine is printed frequently, this is an option. Short corrections can be offered in a simple sentence or two (see Figure 5.17). Such corrections usually appear somewhere in the magazine's introductory material. Errata should be short and direct.

If the major error makes a work difficult to read, you might choose to reprint the entire work in your next issue, heading the reprint with an editor's note such as: "The MEMORIX Staff regrets errors in printing 'Actually Affluent' in our March issue. The essay is reprinted below for your enjoyment."

Insert Sheet

An insert sheet offers immediate correction of an error. For annual publications, this may be the only practical means of correction. Speed is important here; the magazine is ready for distribution or on sale and you do not want the process held up.

To ready an errata insert sheet, type out the errata, being as brief and direct as possible. Omissions or reversals of lines might best be handled by reprinting the entire stanza, paragraph, or section affected (see Figure 5.18).

Figure 5.18
Errata Insert Sheet

> **Errata**
>
> The photograph on page 38 is by Troy Hernandez.
> The final stanza of "Anxiety," on page 15, should read
> > Reaffirm Ridiculous Roles
> > Define Different Desires
> > Sense Something Special
> > Mean Maybe More
>
> The UNICORN Staff regrets these errors.

Next, reproduce the errata insert sheet by whatever means are quick, inexpensive, and available. Cut the insert sheets to a size that will easily slip inside your magazine. Finally, stuff an errata sheet in each magazine. If there is time and a place in the magazine that is not too distracting, you may want to attach (glue, tape, staple) the errata sheet so that it does not fall out.

A final note: Errata are not totally unexpected, but major errors should not be the norm, either. If your staff is handling several items of errata for every issue, review your proofreading process; it is letting you down.

MORGUE DAY

Your magazine will be done, a victory in itself, but your magazine also will be really done, meaning that no further changes can be made or ideas added. With this in mind, journalists have an event called *morgue day*, the day after an issue is published, when the staff analyzes the results. You will want to discuss your successes and analyze problems that need to be solved for future issues. Don't forget to celebrate!

To thoughts about morgue day, add this thought of Emily Dickinson's:

> A word is dead
> When it is said,
>   Some say.
> I say it just
> Begins to live
>   That day.

Don't forget to celebrate!

Questions and Activities

1. Make a list of items to check on a final layout. Compare your listing with other staff members' and compile a master list for your staff.
2. At this point in your magazine's production schedule, you are nearly done but may have layouts to check, a publicity campaign to launch, and final evaluations of your magazine to consider. What are two actions you can take to lower your stress level and focus your energies on the remaining tasks?

APPENDIXES

(A) SAMPLE MANUSCRIPTS

You may find any number of uses for the following manuscripts. They might be used as samples on which to test your evaluation forms before critiquing manuscripts of your own. You might also debate possible titles for these works, discuss the possibilities for illustration that each offers, consider whether any would benefit from revision, or practice grouping them for double-page spreads. Some of the following are by professional writers, others, by students. Authors' names are listed on the acknowledgments page of this book.

Manuscript #1

There is only the rise and fall
as the meters slowly descend
and never enough have passed
before the rise begins again

And every continuing collision
leaves your shins in painful
                              splinters
your muscles in steel torrents
as your feet fall in snowy winter

But sometimes, in puddles of Spring
when rainbows lie under the clouds
There's only that special feeling
                              you love
and the admiration of the crowds

But most of the time it seems
there's only the echo of worn stone

as your agonizing steps connect
when you run through the streets
                              alone

And only when you break the tape
and you've finally outrun time
you touch your dream for a
                              moment . . .
but dreams never have finish lines.
—dedicated in most loving memory
to Coach Don Osse, 1936–1985

Manuscript #2

Come, my love,
to a land long ago,
Where the sunshine is bright
and cool waters flow.

In our own special place,
now together at last,
as each and every day
becomes one of the past.

We come just as close
as true lovers can
with kisses so sweet
of ancient woman and man.

Manuscript #3

Apples are red.
This I know because I'm told—
unless they're green
which depends on the variety.
Though some are yellow
Because it is willed.
Yet others are brown
But not intentionally.

Just as,
People are good
as my mother once said.
Unless they are bad—
Which depends on the cause.
Though some are justified
Because it is willed.
Yet others are damned
But not intentionally.

Manuscript #4

I, for one, am going to know what to say when the ducks show up. I've made a list of phrases, and although I don't know which one to use yet, they are all good enough in case they showed up tomorrow. Many people won't know what to say when the ducks show up, but I will. Maybe I'll say, "Oh, ducks, oh ducks, oh ducks," or just "ducks, wonderful ducks!" I practice these sayings every day, and even though the ducks haven't come yet, when they do, I'll know what to say.

Manuscript #5

I think that I shall never see
A billboard lovely as a tree.
Indeed, unless the billboards fall
I'll never see a tree at all.

Manuscript #6

It was hot, the heated stone burned my bare feet as I walked up the great Aztec pyramid. I felt weak, about to collapse. I reached forward and crawled nearer to my destination. The sun, beating against my back, made my whole body thirst. Only five more steps. My feet, burned and frazzled, dragged along the stone as my hands pulled my limp body up the steps. Now, my hands had reached the top. There, slouched over the hot stone, I recalled the goal of my journey. I reached into my pocket and drew out three silver coins. My weakened hand groped for the slot. There was a rumble, a crashing sound. I took the ice cold Pepsi.

Manuscript #7

Last year at Awards time, two or three people picked most of them up. Their works were indeed superior and the judges had little choice. But this year at Awards time, the men in tuxedos and women in gowns of exotic cloths and laces heard an even, if not odd, distribution of prizes. The administrators at first gave reasons for certain awards, as though making excuses for decisions of which they were once confident.

"The MacFarland award to Mister Falcon because he spent a lot of time summarizing first."

The room was a murmur and Falcon stood up and marched toward the stage and his coat-tails brushed the oak of the walls of this old building.

Then Jackson was given the prize of distinguished accomplishment. The crowd lowly gumbled and a few peripheral members applauded. The judges seemed defiant, as though they were acting on new information.

The judges continued passing awards out to unlikely people, and favorites were acclaimed in categories they never expected.

And so for forty-five minutes the crowd sat astonished and listened to judges announcing awards for stature and flow of line.

I think that after the first thirty minutes, the members, now mellowed by wine, began to understand and rejoice in the course of the evening and conversation and wit were heard in the room with the dim chandeliers. Then everyone picked up their wraps and awards, walked outside in the light snow, departed in carriages, or some in their cars, and vanished into a black night, thinking of something they knew long ago.

Manuscript #8

When all in silks my Julia goes,
Then, then, I think, how sweetly
            flows
That liquifaction of her clothes.

Next, when I cast my eyes, and see
That brave vibration, each way
            free,
O, how that glittering does take me!

Manuscript #9

She sits next to me, yawning from her loss of sleep last night. I'm already sure what she'll say:

"Ooooohhh, I'm so tired." She looks at me in a sad sort of way, hoping I'll comfort her . . . but I won't.

With a small grin she places her legs on mine, using me for a footstool. She runs her fingers gently down my arm, hoping I'll get excited . . . but I won't. Her flirting increases as she thinks of an excuse to reach in my pocket.

Teasing her I say, "So when are we gonna go out and have some *real* fun?"

"Anytime," she replies casually, with a lustful smile. She thinks I'll get turned on . . . but I won't.

Unconsciously, I stare at her body. I look at her face, slightly accented with make-up. Her hair is long and full. Her eyes, dark and hypnotizing, stare into mine, and her face moves closer to mine. Her lips, wet and glistening from a light shade of lipstick. I wonder what she's thinking. She wonders the same

thing. She thinks I'll say something first . . . but I won't.

Breaking the silence, she tells me of a party she was at last night: "Too bad you weren't there; it might have been more fun." The smile reappears.

The bell rings, and she waits for me to get up. We walk into the hall together, silent. She struts down the hall in a sophisticated manner. She thinks I'll fall in love with her . . . and I won't.

(B) RATINGS AND EVALUATIONS

Throughout your production schedule, you will peer into the future, defining and bringing into focus a magazine no one has ever seen before. Through meetings and work sessions you will feel it grow. When you hold it in your hands for the first time, you will probably feel like a new parent. And whether it is absolutely wonderful or not, it is yours.

After the newness has worn off, you will probably ask yourself, "How good is our magazine?" First, give yourself credit for having completed a significant, creative product. That is success in itself. Then, your staff will want to conduct its own evaluation. Return to your staff's goals, as established in Chapter 1. What questions can you ask yourselves that will tell you whether your magazine achieved its goals? Perhaps you will also seek feedback from the student body, faculty members, and community members whose opinion the staff respects. Once you have studied this textbook and produced a magazine, you will know what aspects of your own magazine are important to evaluate.

Finally, although your own evaluation is the most important one, you may want to consider submitting your magazine to a rating service or contest. Such services can offer you a broadly based perspective on the standards your magazine has achieved. In addition to organizations you may know of in your area, a number of national organizations operate contests for literary magazines and literary-art magazines. These services issue awards, and most offer written critiques of your magazine. Write for information soon, so that your school will be on their mailing lists in time to receive applications and be notified of deadlines.

National Rating Services

American Scholastic Press Association Contest/Review
Box 4400
College Point, NY 11356

Columbia Scholastic Press Association Contest/Critique
Box 11, Central Mail Room
Columbia University
New York, NY 10027-6969

Program to Recognize Excellence in Student Literary Magazines
National Council of Teachers of English
1111 Kenyon Road
Urbana, IL 61801

The National Scholastic Press Association
All American Critical Service
620 Rarig Center
330 21st Avenue South
University of Minnesota
Minneapolis, MN 55455

(C) WORKLOAD CHART

On an 18-week production schedule, this chart shows possible deadlines and involvement with the three basic functions every literary magazine staff must handle.

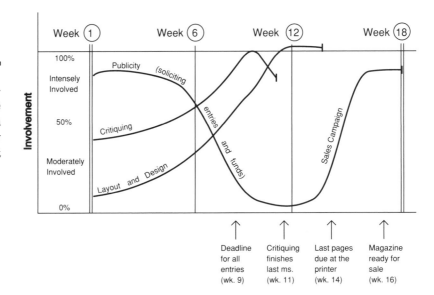

GLOSSARY

CREATIVE WRITERS', JOURNALISTS', AND PRINTERS' TERMS

Terms related to creative writing are marked with an asterisk (*). This glossary contains many creative writing terms that do not appear in the text but appear here for ready reference in discussing literature.

Abstract art: Art in which the subject has been reduced or abstracted to focus on a particular aspect of it. Examples: *Broadway Boogie-Woogie* (Mondrian), the NBC peacock. See *non-objective art, subject*.

All caps (caps and caps): Instruction to a typesetter to set with all capital letters of the same size.

Allegory: Literary or art work in which characters, objects, and events operate as symbols commenting on an idea or principle. An allegory operates on both a literal and a symbolic level. Examples: *Animal Farm* (Orwell), *The Little Prince* (Saint-Exupéry).

Alliteration: Repetition of initial consonant sounds. Sometimes repeated initial *vowel* sounds also are termed alliteration ("All of Achille's armor"). Example: "Grendel/ Went up to Herot, *w*ondering *w*hat the warriors/ Would do . . ." (*Beowulf*, trans. Raffel). See *partial rhyme, consonance, assonance*.

Alphabet poem: (1) Poem spelling out a word vertically with the first letter of each line; acrostic. (2) Poem based on the letters of the alphabet: "*A*lways *b*egin *c*ounting *d*ucks whose *e*very *f*light . . ."

Amberlith: See *rubylith*.

Ambiguous: Subject to multiple, sometimes uncertain, interpretations.

Anchor: Literary or art work of high quality and general appeal placed at a strategic position in a magazine to draw readers to it.

Antagonist: Any person, being, or force that works to keep the protagonists from reaching their goal. In complicated stories, there may be more than one antagonist. Examples: the Joker in *Batman*; social prejudices, unjust laws, the Duke and Dauphin in *Huckleberry Finn*. See *protagonist*.

Approximate rhyme: See *partial rhyme*.

Assonance: Repetition of vowel sounds. Examples: slapdash, grave/ vein, heart/farm. See *consonance, alliteration, partial rhyme*.

Ballad: Narrative poem written in stanzas, often with one stanza repeated as a chorus or refrain and often meant to be sung. Examples: "Barbara Allen," "The Wreck of the *Edmund Fitzgerald*."

Black space: Space on a page that is filled with titles, borders, lines, bold-faced type, photos, or artwork. See *gray space, white space*.

Blank verse: See *iambic pentameter*.

Bleed: To place printed illustrations or ornamentation so as to run off the page in one or more directions.

Blueline: See *proof*.

Body type: Small type, usually 8 to 10 points, in which most of a publication's copy is set.

Burnish: To rub any paper attached to a layout as a way of assuring that it does not come off. Typeset copy and artwork is always protected with an additional piece of paper while doing this.

C-1, C-2, C-3, C-4: Numbering system for a magazine's front cover (C-1), inside front cover (C-2), inside back cover (C-3), and back cover (C-4) when the cover is of a different paper stock than the body of the magazine.

Camera-ready copy (photo-ready copy, final pasteup): Text and artwork in final form, completely prepared for a printer's camera. A printing plate is made from the negative of this copy.

Caps: Abbreviation for capital letters. See *all caps*.

Caps and l.c.: Instruction to a typesetter to set capital letters followed by lowercase letters.

Caps and s.c.: Instruction to a typesetter to set with capital letters followed by smaller capital letters.

*Cliché: Overused phrase or idea. Popular similes or alliterative phrases often become clichés. Examples: "Through thick and thin," "Take it lying down," "School of hard knocks," "As clear as mud."

*Climax: In fiction, the highest point of the action, the point at which the reader knows whether the protagonist wins or loses. Examples: When the woodsman storms into Grandma's house in "Little Red Riding Hood"; when Wilson shoots Gatsby in *The Great Gatsby*.

Colophon: (1) Description giving facts about a magazine's publication. (2) Publisher's logo or emblem, usually placed on the title page.

Column inch: Space one column wide and one vertical inch long.

Comb binding: Binding in which a plastic, many-toothed, rolled comb is inserted into a series of holes punched along the vertical edge of a stack of loose sheets.

*Concrete poetry: Poetry in which words, type, and white space are arranged so that the poem's shape is a direct part of its meaning.
Example: book page book book book
           back book book book book
           glue book book bookbrick

*Conflict: In fiction, the clash of actions, goals, philosophies, or emotions that keep the protagonist from reaching her goal. Traditionally, conflicts are classified as humans vs. humans, humans vs. themselves, humans vs. society, humans vs. nature, or humans vs. the unknown (fate).

*Consonance: Repetition of final (terminal) consonant sounds. Examples: odds/ends, rain/tone. Often combined with alliteration: crisscross, book/brick. See *partial rhyme, assonance, alliteration*.

Copyright: Authors' or artists' right to control publication of their works.

Correction fluid (opaquing fluid): White liquid that paints over typing errors and smudges on a layout without being picked up by the printer's camera.

Cover stock: Paper used for a magazine's cover that is heavier than paper for the text.

Credit: Author's or artist's name appearing adjacent to his work.

Crop: To eliminate for printing unwanted area in an artwork.

Deadline: Time before which something must be done; latest possible time at which material can be accepted. Example: the day and time at which material must be ready for the printer.

Denouement (resolution): [´day new maw] In fiction, the wrapping up of details necessary to end the story. Example: Gatsby's funeral (*The Great Gatsby*).

*Derivative literature: Literature or art that is merely a take-off or mimicry of another work's structure or style. See *parody*.

Desktop publishing: Use of personal computers to assist in laying out and typesetting printed products.

*Deus ex machina: [day ´oos ex maw´keen ah] Any artificial or forced element (person, object, event) introduced unexpectedly to resolve the difficulties of a plot. Such endings are unsatisfying. Examples: "And just as the monster sensed my presence and turned toward me, I woke up and realized it had all been a dream." "Little did Jason know that the strange letter he was about to open contained a check from the estate of a distant relative."

Die cut: (*n.*) Hole cut in one page to frame part of the image on the page beneath. (*v.*) To cut such a hole.

*Direct characterization: Character development in which the author describes the nature of the character directly to the reader, without calling for interpretation. Example: "Jim often had trouble making up his mind, even about simple things." See *indirect characterization*.

Dominance: Quality of a well-designed spread in which one larger element, usually an artwork or title, draws the reader's eyes to it because of size or position.

Double burn: Instruction to the printer to make one negative of two image areas laid one on top of the other. Common use is to place copy so that it appears in the image area of a photo or artwork.

Dummy: See *mock-up*.

*Dynamic character: Character who changes significantly as a result of the events of the plot. Examples: John and Elizabeth Proctor (*The Crucible*), Jonah and Samson (Bible). See *static character*.

*Empathy: In literature, caring for or responding emotionally to a character. When an author can evoke empathy, the characters begin to come alive for the reader.

*Epistolary story: Prose form in which a story is told entirely through a series of letters. Examples: *The Color Purple* (Walker), *Daddy Long Legs* (Webster).

*Euphemism: Inoffensive expression used in place of one that might be offensive or unpleasant. While euphemisms may allow authors tact in discussing sensitive issues, euphemisms also tend to be vague and are often clichés. Examples: "He has left us," a mortuary's *slumber room*, "Join us for *cocktails*," "She's *in a family way*."

*Exposition: In fiction, material introducing the characters, setting the scene, and giving necessary background information.

External margin: Space between a work (art or literature) and the edge of the page. See *internal margin*.

*Eye rhyme: See *sight rhyme*.

*Falling action: In fiction, events after the climax and before the denouement.

Family: Name of all the typefaces in a particular style. Examples: Bauhaus, Souvenir, English Times.

*Figurative language: Language with two or more levels of meaning; language that cannot be taken literally. See *literal language*.

Filler: Any brief bit of information used to fill space in a spread. More common in newspapers than in magazines.

*Final pasteup: See *camera-ready copy*.

*Fixed form: Any subgenre of poetry with standard rules for its construction. Examples: haiku, limerick, sonnet.

Flat: One-half of a signature, often four pages. A flat is either the up-side or the down-side of the signature as it goes through the press. See *signature*.

*Flat (two-dimensional) character: Character with few differentiating, individual characteristics. See *round character*.

Flop: Instruction to a printer to turn over a negative so that images on the left appear on the right and vice-versa.

Flush left: Typesetting in which the first letters of the lines form a straight line on the left-hand side of the copy. The right edge remains ragged. Flush right copy is uncommon, but possible. See *justified copy*.

Folio line (running head or foot): Line of type on each text page giving the page number, date, and name of the magazine. Page numbers alone are known as *folios*.

*Forced rhyme: Rhyme that calls attention to itself by awkward grammar or unnatural word order. Forced rhymes can occur when the author chooses a word because it fits a needed rhyme scheme rather than because it communicates purposefully. Example: Little grubby hands with dirt and soot,/Up with which she would not put.

*Foreshadowing: In many genres, basic technique for building suspense in which the author hints at events to come. Ranges from obvious statements like "Little did he know what lay ahead" to subtle symbols that appear at significant times.

Format: Magazine's general appearance as determined by its physical size and organization.

*Free verse: Poetry with structure determined by the subject material and needs of the author, rather than by any predetermined rules or forms. Free verse does not have a regular rhythm (meter) and usually does not rhyme. Examples: works by T. S. Eliot, e. e. cummings, Gwendolyn Brooks.

*Genre: [zhan´ruh] Major category of artistic expression, marked by an identifiable form, style, or content. In literature, the genres by form are poetry, drama, short story, novel, and essay. See *subgenre*.

Glue-bound (perfect-bound): Binding in which pages are glued to a cloth or paper backing, forming a hard, flat spine as found on a paperback book.

Graphic: (*adj.*) Bold; clearly outlined, without gray areas. Examples: a *graphic* description of the scene; a *graphic* page layout. (*n.*) An element of a spread that helps direct the flow of a page, such as type, lines, dots, or curves.

Graphics (graphic arts): (1) Any artform, such as etching or woodcut, that involves reproduction from a block or plate. (2) Arts of painting, drawing, and printmaking.

Gray space: Space on a page that is filled with body type. See *white space, black space*.

Gutter: Vertical margin between facing pages of a spread.

*Haiku: Unrhymed, unmetered three-line poem originating from the Japanese and focusing often on a single detail of nature. It relies on understatement, subtlety, and suggestion for its success. In its most rigid form, haiku consists of 17 syllables arranged 5, 7, 5. Longer syllable-based poems are the tanka (5, 7, 5, 7, 7) and the cinquain (2, 4, 6, 8, 2).

Halftone: Process, metal plate, or print in which gradation of tone (white to gray to black) is obtained by a system of small dots produced by photographing through a fine screen.

*Iambic pentameter: Most common meter in English poetry, consisting of five iambs per line. An iamb consists of an unaccented syllable followed by an accented one (*alike, resolve, disgrace*). Unrhymed iambic pentameter is called *blank verse*. Example: "When in disgrace with Fortune and men's eyes" (Shakespeare). See *metered verse*.

*Incidents of complication: Problems, complications, or "roadblocks" that impede the resolution of the conflict in a work of fiction. Example: Bob is rushing his pregnant wife to the hospital 150 miles away when he realizes he needs gas, and the one local station is closed.

*Inciting incident (exciting force): Incident or circumstance that begins the conflict in a work of fiction. Examples: A tornado warning is announced on the radio; Jill asks Jack to marry her; Herman discovers that his friend lied to him.

*Indirect characterization: Character development in which the author describes a character's thoughts and actions and allows the reader to infer the nature of the character. Example: "Jim sat on the edge of the bed, wondering what to put on first—his pants or his socks." See *direct characterization*.

Internal margin: Space between works (art or literature) on a page. See *external margin*.

Internal quote (callout): Excerpt of body copy repeated in the layout in larger type to draw readers into the copy.

*Irony: Language or circumstance involving an incongruity; the expected sequence is somehow twisted. Irony may occur in art, but is most common in literature.

Verbal irony occurs when a writer says the opposite of what he means and what is expected. In complex examples, the author means both what she says *and* the opposite. Example: "I've got bad news—he'll live."

Dramatic irony occurs when the audience or reader knows something unknown to one or more characters. Example: In *Arsenic and Old Lace*, a policeman enters a house where the audience has just seen a corpse hidden in a window seat. In casual conversation the officer sits there, saying that his job often brings him close to death.

Circumstantial irony (irony of situation) involves a twisted difference between what would be expected to happen and what actually comes to happen. Example: King Midas is granted his wish: everything he touches turns to gold; but "everything" includes his food, and he cannot eat.

Issue: Particular, dated copy of a periodical. Example: The December issue of *Life*. See *volume*.

Jump: (*v.*) To continue a work in another location, usually at the back of the magazine. (*n.*) Portion of the work continued.

Justified copy: Lines of type set so that the left and right margins form straight edges. See *flush left*.

Layout: Sketch or plan that indicates to the staff or printer how copy and visual materials will be arranged in a spread.

Layout sheet: Paper backing, usually marked to show margins and gutter, on which a final pasteup is done. See *mounting board*.

Leading: [led′ing] In typeset copy, space added between lines; originally created with lead.

Libel: In writing, unjust damage to someone's reputation.

Line shot: Straight camera shot for printing made without use of a halftone screen. A line shot will appear as black and white only, without gray.

*Literal language: Words used as they are commonly used; language conforming to dictionary definitions; language without double meanings. See *figurative language*.

Logo: (1) Symbol which represents a business. Examples: McDonald's golden arches, Subaru's six stars. (2) Distinctive treatment of a business's name. For examples, see the *New York Times*, Levi's, Pepsi, Coke. (3) A colophon.

Lowercase: Small letters; not capital letters.

Masthead: (1) Listing of information about the magazine, staff, and publisher. (2) Newspaper's name, as seen at the top of the front page.

Media: Newspapers, television, magazines, or other means for mass communication.

Medium: Particular artistic technique determined by the materials required. Examples: watercolor, marble, oil paint. Words are the medium of literature.

*Metaphor: Comparison of two basically unlike things without the use of *like*, *as*, or *than*. Metaphors, similes, and personification are all figures of speech that can be extended through a paragraph, stanza, or entire work. Example: "Camille's hair was a bird's nest long abandoned." See *simile*.

*Metered verse: Poetry based on a regular rhythm pattern of accented and unaccented syllables. Examples: limerick, sonnet. See *iambic pentameter*.

*Mixed metaphor: Incongruous image produced in a metaphor; not desirable unless for humorous effect. Example: "His enthusiasm was corralled by a wave of opposition."

Mock-up (dummy): A model of a magazine that records the placement of the components in the magazine. When used as the editor's book, a mock-up also records the status of each spread.

*Mood: General atmosphere of a story or poem, often developed through the setting and choice of language. Both mood and tone are expressed as adjectives. Examples: *Les Miserables* (oppressive, yearning, chaotic, dark, fateful), *You're a Good Man, Charlie Brown* (whimsical, light, innocent, warm). See *tone*.

*Moral: Basic rule or philosophy for living stated as the purpose of a literary work, often a fable. Examples: "Don't count your chickens before they're hatched"; "The grass is always greener on the other side."

Mounting board: Heavyweight paper backing, usually marked to show gutter and margins, on which final pasteups are done. See *layout sheet*.

*Narrative focus: In any story, detail with which the author portrays events and people. The three narrative focuses may be compared to the movement of a movie camera in the following way:

Description: Author stops the action, aiming her camera directly at what she wants the reader to see and detailing what the camera frames. Example: "Julia's big honest face hung out like a neon sign. 'Love me.' her big green eyes blinked, 'I need love.'"

Summary: Author pans quickly over the action, condensing time and space. Example: "Julia's brother set up her last date for her. Julia had met the guy at a restaurant and, after ordering, he disappeared into the men's restroom. Permanently."

Scene: Author tracks the action at almost the actual speed it occurred. Example: "Jaime pulled out a chair for his date and smiled as he handed her a menu. 'Please don't disappear like the last one,' Julia thought as he rounded the table and took his own seat."

Non-exclusive rights: Category of copyright law in which an author grants permission to print a work of his in the current and future issues of a periodical. See *one-time rights*.

Nonobjective art: Art without a subject; sometimes called *abstract*. Music, painting, or sculpture may or may not have subjects. Examples: *Fifth Symphony* (Beethoven), *Painting no. 201* (Kandinsky). See *subject, abstract art*.

Non-photo: Inks, pens, and pencils that allow designers to draw guidelines or write instructions that are not "seen" when photographed. Commonly blue.

One-time rights: Category of copyright law in which an author grants permission for a work to be printed in only one issue of a periodical. See *non-exclusive rights*.

*Onomatopoeia: Use of words intended to sound like what they mean. Examples: *buzz, click,* and *wham*; "the silken sad uncertain rustling of each purple curtain" (Poe).

Opaquing fluid: See *correction fluid*.

*Organic structure: Structure, in poetry or prose, determined by the subject material and needs of the author, rather than by any predetermined rules or forms. Examples: sketches, think pieces, free verse.

*Overstatement (hyperbole): Representation, for the purpose of emphasis, of something as more than it really is. Be aware of overstatements which have become clichés: "If I've told you once, I've told you a thousand times . . . ." Example: "The line for tickets stretched unendingly from the box office." See *understatement*.

*Parody: Literary or art work that successfully mixes mimicry and originality so that the work mimicked is held up for comic effect or ridicule. See *derivative literature*.

*Partial rhyme (approximate rhyme, slant rhyme): Sound elements that can tie ideas together and create subtle secondary meanings. Though typically associated with poetry, they can be used effectively in prose as well. Examples: alliteration, consonance, assonance. See *alliteration, assonance, consonance*.

Percentage wheel (proportion wheel, sizing wheel): Tool allowing a designer to determine the percent by which an item is to be enlarged or reduced to fit into a layout.

Perfect-bound: See *glue-bound*.

*Personification: Figurative language in which human characteristics are given to an object, animal, or idea. Example: "I am silver and exact. I have no preconceptions" ("Mirror" by Plath).

Pica: Printer's unit of measure equal to one-sixth inch; usually measured horizontally. See *point*.

Plagiarism: The act of claiming another's words or ideas as your own.

*Plot: In fiction, plan or main story; involves a problem solved, or at least confronted.

Point: Printer's unit of measure equal to one-twelfth pica; usually measured vertically. See *pica*.

***Point of view**: Narrator's position relative to the action of a story.

In *first-person* point of view, narrator is a character in the action.

In *third-person dramatic* point of view, narrator observes the action and reports what the characters do and say but does not interpret actions or reveal private thoughts.

In *third-person omniscient* point of view, narrator can reveal what characters say, do, think, and feel, as well as declare reasons for their actions. The omniscient point of view can be limited, so that the narrator reveals the inner thoughts and feelings of only one character.

In *stream-of-consciousness* point of view, narrator reveals his thoughts as they are heard inside his head, without organizing them into sentences or giving them formal structure.

***Portmanteau word**: Word blending syllables and meanings of two other words. Examples: *smog* (*smoke* + *fog*), *chortle* (*chuckle* + *snort*).

Practice pasteup: "Dry run" in which designer places photocopies of the page parts on a layout sheet at actual size, in preparation for completing the camera-ready copy or final layout. See *camera-ready copy*.

Presstype (rub-off letters): Purchased lettering available in many styles and sizes that can be transferred to a layout for titles and other uses. Common brands: Format, Chartpack, Lettraset.

Proof (silver print, blueline): (*n.*) Printed test-sheet of a page made to check for printer's errors. (*v.*) To check copy or layouts for mechanical errors.

Proportion wheel: See *percentage wheel*.

***Prose**: Writing that is not poetry.

***Protagonist**: In fiction, person or being for whom the conflict exists. See *antagonist*.

***Pseudonym**: Fictitious name taken by an author; pen name.

Reader service: Any component of a magazine that aids readers in understanding the format and accessing the content. Examples: table of contents, folio line, artists' and authors' credits.

***Resolution**: See *denouement*.

Reverse: Instruction to printer to reverse a negative, so that white areas are black and black areas, white.

Revision: (1) Final version of a manuscript altered in form or content by the author or staff. (2) Portion of a manuscript so altered. See *proof*.

***Rhyme (full rhyme, perfect rhyme)**: (*v.*) Matching of terminal sounds (consonants and vowels) in two or more words; assonance + consonance = rhyme. Examples: bone/stone, fairly/rarely, spice/entice. See *partial rhyme*. (*n.*) Poem having full rhyme. See *partial rhyme*.

***Rising action**: Building of one event upon another, leading to the climax in a work of fiction.

Rough (dummy, preliminary): Initial sketch of a layout, showing the placement of basic page components.

***Round (three-dimensional) character**: Fully developed character with many unique, individualized characteristics. See *flat character*.

Rubylith/Amberlith: Special purpose photographic mediums that allow a visual area to be eliminated or identified for special treatment.

Running head: See *folio line*.

Saddle stitching: See *staple binding*.

Sans serif: Style of lettering without serifs.

***Satire**: Literature in which human habits, follies, or failings are held up to ridicule. Satire's serious purpose is to bring about reform or keep others from failing. Examples: *Gulliver's Travels* (Swift), *Animal Farm* (Orwell).

Screen: To use a screen (a transparent plate with dots) in a photographic process. Most common use is in halftones.

***Sentimentality**: Contrived emotion; in a literary or art work, that which seeks to bring tears by oversimplifying or distorting.

Serif: A smaller line used to finish off a main stroke in a letter. The letters you are reading have serifs.

Service bureau: Business offering camera and copy printing services to aid designers in readying layouts for a printer.

***Sight rhyme (eye rhyme)**: At the ends of words, matching of spelling not matched in sound. Examples: *through/rough, lint/pint, have/grave*.

Signature: Large paper sheet which, when folded into pages and combined with other signatures for binding, forms a magazine or book. See *flat*.

Silver print: See *proof*.

***Simile**: Comparison of two basically unlike things with the use of *like, as*, or *than*. Example: "He was as strong as yesterday's socks." See *metaphor*.

***Sketch**: Short prose form in which the author "sketches" (describes, portrays) a person or place.

*Slant rhyme: See *partial rhyme*.

*Sonnet: Fourteen-line poem in iambic pentameter; Italian and English variations exist. Examples: sonnets of Shakespeare or E. B. Browning.

Spine: Hinge-like back edge of a magazine or book.

Spread (double-page spread): Two facing pages in a magazine handled visually as a single unit.

*Stanza: Unit of a poem, somewhat equivalent to a paragraph in prose. Stanzas often share number of lines, rhythm, and rhyme.

Staple binding (saddle stitching, wiring): Binding in which two or three staples through the spine secure the pages.

*Static character: Character whose personality, values, and goals are essentially unchanged by the events of the plot. Examples: Abraham (Bible), Superman. See *dynamic character*.

Stylebook (style sheet): Written guide that lists a magazine's rules for mechanics and style.

*Subgenre: Subdivision of a genre. Although not appearing in many dictionaries, *subgenre* is useful in describing smaller categories of literature. Examples: science fiction, mystery, narrative poetry, personal essay. See *genre*.

*Subject: That which a work is about; what a work represents. Literature almost always has a subject. Examples: the American Revolution (*Johnny Tremain*), a Grecian urn (Keats's "Ode"). See *abstract art, non-objective art, theme*.

*Surprise ending: Story resolution that comes upon the reader as a surprise. A good surprise ending will startle at first, but seem logical after consideration.

Teasers: Short messages, literary excerpts, or small pictures on a magazine's cover, title page, or table of contents that lure readers into the magazine. Also called *ears* when placed in the upper corners of a newspaper's front page.

*Theme: Literary work's main idea; what the author says about the subject. A complicated, longer work may have more than one theme. Examples: War can divide even the closest families; The unpredictable power of nature causes people to contemplate the nature of God's power. See *subject*.

*Tone: Author's attitude toward her subject; emotional overtones. Tone and mood are often the same, but not necessarily. Strong mood and tone are points for a story or poem. Example: The mood of the TV series "The Addams Family" is eerie and haunting, but the tone is humorous. See *mood*.

Trapped white space: On a page, unprinted space wider than the internal margin and bounded on three or four sides by copy or artwork.

*Understatement: Representation of something as less than it really is for the purpose, ironically, of emphasis. Example: He faced the reconstruction of an entire factory destroyed by the hurricane, but only said "This will be a challenge." See *overstatement*.

Volume: (1) Year of a periodical's life. (2) The compilation of all of a periodical's issues in a year. See *issue*.

White space: Unprinted space on a page, regardless of the paper's color. See *gray space, black space*.

Window: Clear opening in a printer's negative for positioning of a second negative, usually of artwork.

INDEX

NTC LANGUAGE ARTS BOOKS

Business Communication
Business Communication Today! *Thomas & Fryar*
Handbook for Business Writing, *Baugh, Fryar, & Thomas*
Meetings: Rules & Procedures, *Pohl*

Dictionaries
British/American Language Dictionary, *Moss*
NTC's Classical Dictionary, *Room*
NTC's Dictionary of Changes in Meaning, *Room*
NTC's Dictionary of Debate, *Hanson*
NTC's Dictionary of Literary Terms, *Morner & Rausch*
NTC's Dictionary of Theatre and Drama Terms, *Mobley*
NTC's Dictionary of Word Origins, *Room*
NTC's Spell It Right Dictionary, *Downing*
Robin Hyman's Dictionary of Quotations

Essential Skills
Building Real Life English Skills, *Starkey & Penn*
English Survival Series, *Maggs*
Essential Life Skills, *Starkey & Penn*
Essentials of English Grammar, *Baugh*
Essentials of Reading and Writing English Series
Grammar for Use, *Hall*
Grammar Step-by-Step, *Pratt*
Guide to Better English Spelling, *Furness*
How to be a Rapid Reader, *Redway*
How to Improve Your Study Skills, *Coman & Heavers*
NTC Skill Builders
Reading by Doing, *Simmons & Palmer*
Developing Creative & Critical Thinking, *Boostrom*
303 Dumb Spelling Mistakes, *Downing*
TIME: We the People, *ed. Schinke-Llano*
Vocabulary by Doing, *Beckert*

Genre Literature
The Detective Story, *Schwartz*
The Short Story & You, *Simmons & Stern*
Sports in Literature, *Emra*
You and Science Fiction, *Hollister*

Journalism
Getting Started in Journalism, *Harkrider*
Journalism Today! *Ferguson & Patten*
Publishing the Literary Magazine, *Klaiman*
UPI Stylebook, *United Press International*

Language, Literature, and Composition
An Anthology for Young Writers, *Meredith*
The Art of Composition, *Meredith*
Creative Writing, *Mueller & Reynolds*

Handbook for Practical Letter Writing, *Baugh*
How to Write Term Papers and Reports, *Baugh*
Literature by Doing, *Tchudi & Yesner*
Lively Writing, *Schrank*
Look, Think & Write, *Leavitt & Sohn*
Poetry by Doing, *Osborn*
World Literature, *Rosenberg*
Write to the Point! *Morgan*
The Writer's Handbook, *Karls & Szymanski*
Writing by Doing, *Sohn & Enger*
Writing in Action, *Meredith*

Media Communication
Getting Started in Mass Media, *Beckert*
Photography in Focus, *Jacobs & Kokrda*
Television Production Today! *Kirkham*
Understanding Mass Media, *Schrank*
Understanding the Film, *Bone & Johnson*

Mythology
The Ancient World, *Sawyer & Townsend*
Mythology and You, *Rosenberg & Baker*
Welcome to Ancient Greece, *Millard*
Welcome to Ancient Rome, *Millard*
World Mythology, *Rosenberg*

Speech
Activities for Effective Communication, *LiSacchi*
The Basics of Speech, *Galvin, Cooper, & Gordon*
Contemporary Speech, *HopKins & Whitaker*
Dynamics of Speech, *Myers & Herndon*
Getting Started in Public Speaking, *Prentice & Payne*
Listening by Doing, *Galvin*
Literature Alive! *Gamble & Gamble*
Person to Person, *Galvin & Book*
Public Speaking Today! *Prentice & Payne*
Speaking by Doing, *Buys, Sill, & Beck*

Theatre
Acting & Directing, *Grandstaff*
The Book of Cuttings for Acting & Directing, *Cassady*
The Book of Scenes for Acting Practice, *Cassady*
The Dynamics of Acting, *Snyder & Drumsta*
An Introduction to Modern One-Act Plays, *Cassady*
An Introduction to Theatre and Drama, *Cassady & Cassady*
Play Production Today! *Beck et al.*
Stagecraft, *Beck*

For a current catalog and information about our complete line
of language arts books, write:
National Textbook Company
a division of NTC Publishing Group
4255 West Touhy Avenue
Lincolnwood (Chicago), Illinois 60646-1975 U.S.A.